MEDITATIONS
ON
EARLY
CHRISTIAN
SYMBOLS

abingdon press ♪ new york . nashville

MEDITATIONS
ON
EARLY
CHRISTIAN
SYMBOLS

MICHAEL DAVES

MEDITATIONS ON EARLY CHRISTIAN SYMBOLS

Copyright © 1964 by Abingdon Press

All rights in this book are reserved.
No part of the book may be reproduced in any
manner whatsoever without written permission of
the publishers except brief quotations embodied in
critical articles or reviews. For information address
Abingdon Press, Nashville 2, Tennessee

Library of Congress Catalog Card Number: 64-10600

Quotation on p. 26 from "The Hollow Men"
in Collected Poems of T. S. Eliot, copyright 1936,
by Harcourt, Brace & World, Inc., and reprinted
with their permission, and with the permission of
Faber and Faber, Ltd.

Quotations on pp. 84 and 86-87 from: *The
Unutterable Beauty* by G. A. Studdert-Kennedy.
Copyright by Harper & Row, Publishers, Incorpo-
rated. Used by permission of Harper & Row, Publishers and Hodder & Stoughton, Ltd.

Scripture quotations, unless otherwise noted,
are from the Revised Standard Version of the
Bible, copyrighted 1946 and 1952 by the Division of Christian Education, National Council
of Churches, and are used by permission.

SET UP, PRINTED, AND BOUND BY THE
PARTHENON PRESS, AT NASHVILLE,
TENNESSEE, UNITED STATES OF AMERICA

TO MY WIFE

PREFACE

During one of those rare moments in worship given to the minister to sit and rest, I looked closely at the stained-glass windows of the sanctuary. Each window contained a traditional Christian symbol—the cross, wheat, lamb, anchor, lily, and others. The sun seemed to be shining brighter than usual, and the deep, rich stain of the windows blazed in a cascade of color. Suddenly I realized that here was a parable about the nature of Christian symbols. Our symbols are one way in which God's light shines through upon our lives. Symbols are a major avenue of God's self-disclosure to his covenant community, the church.

Thank God for symbols! Without them, we would be impoverished. Man lives in a material universe, and spiritual reality must be expressed to us in terms of time and space. The Bible is filled with illustrations suggesting the intimate relationship of symbols to faith. The prophets used symbols to make their messages "come alive" for the people. Jeremiah broke an earthen flask as a sign that God would judge

7

swift and sure. Ezekiel made a model of Jerusalem beseiged, lay down beside it, and lived on a starvation diet. This, he predicted, was the bleak future for the city. Hosea symbolized God's judgment on the nation by the names which he gave his children. Jesus Christ was the master of symbols as he rode into Jerusalem on an ass, thus fulfilling ancient prophecy. Earlier, Jesus understood the symbolic nature of the universe: "Consider the lilies of the field, how they grow; they neither toil nor spin; yet I tell you, even Solomon in all his glory was not arrayed like one of these. But if God so clothes the grass of the field, which today is alive and tomorrow is thrown into the oven, will he not much more clothe you, O men of little faith?" (Matt. 6:28-30.) It was a perfectly natural step for the early church to adapt visual symbols to remind them of the God who had encountered them in Jesus Christ.

But Christian symbols are misused, some will object. Yes, and sadly so. Symbols are abused when we forget that they point to a Reality and are not the Reality. For example, the cross symbol is often abused by investing it with magical power instead of allowing it to point to the Christ Event. Recognizing such abuse, many Christians declared war on the traditional symbols and demanded unconditional surrender. Until a generation ago there was not even a cross in many Protestant church buildings, and other traditional symbols were largely unknown.

We are now more aware that it is also an abuse not to use symbols simply on the grounds that they sometimes fall into misuse. To throw out the bath water is one thing, but to throw out the baby with it is plain silly. Today there is a resurgence of Christian symbols in almost every denomi-

8

nation. Building committees want symbols included in plans for the new building. Units of study on symbols are published for the church schools. Church bulletins indicate a new appreciation of symbols as an aid to corporate worship.

Significantly, the renaissance of symbolism began as the church entered into a period of rigorous questioning about its selfhood, a return to biblical theology, a rebirth of the liturgy, and an increased dialogue with all art forms. Symbols help the church to understand what it means to be a Christian community in the twentieth century.

These meditations are designed to stir the imagination and to aid the reader to participate in what the symbols represent. Scripture readings serve as foundation stones for the meditations and also indicate that Christian symbols have their root and ground in the events of Scripture.

—MICHAEL DAVES

CONTENTS

11

VI. MEDITATIONS ON SYMBOLS OF BIBLICAL
DOCTRINES

I

MEDITATIONS ON SYMBOLS
OF GOD THE FATHER

HAND OF GOD

SCRIPTURE   You shall remember that you were a servant in the land of Egypt, and the Lord your God brought you out thence with a mighty hand and an outstretched arm. (Deut. 5:15a.)

> Behold, the Lord's hand is
>   not shortened, that it cannot save,
>   or his ear dull, that it cannot hear. (Isa. 59:1.)

MEDITATION   *David and Lisa* is a film about two emotionally disturbed adolescents and their agonizing struggle for recovery. The drama takes place at a school for mentally disturbed adolescents. David, haunted by fear of death, cannot bear anyone to touch him. Physical touch means death. Lisa is a split personality and speaks in children's rhymes. Prose means more reality than she can endure. The two struggle to make friends. Toward the end of the movie, Lisa runs away from school. David finds her. She looks up into his face and speaks—in prose! David says, "Lisa, you're

17

not rhyming! You're not ryhming!" Slowly, he holds out a trembling hand. "Take my hand, Lisa. . . . *Take my hand.*" As she grasps his hand he knows a moment of intense pain. Then death gives way to life. The two walk away into the morning of a new day, hand in hand.

Hands are vital to communion with one another. We speak with our hands as well as with our mouths. Love, comfort, friendship, beauty, creativity—all come through hands.

Prime Minister Nehru of India keeps a brass mold of Lincoln's right hand on his desk. "A beautiful hand," he says, "strong and firm, yet gentle. I look at it daily and it gives me strength."

The writers of the Bible did not know Lincoln, but they knew about the One who created Lincoln. Remember— they spoke of the hand of God. This metaphor represented God's creative, sustaining attitude toward man. How natural for the early Christians to adopt the hand as a symbol for God. Usually the hand is shown pointing downward from a cloud of glory. This emphasizes God's creativity. Or, the hand may cradle five small figures. This represents God's care. Still another hand is raised in benediction. The fingers are bent so as to form the Greek letters I, C, S, and X, standing for Jesus Christ. This signifies the union of the Father and the Son.

God does not wait for man to make a long, lonely journey to him. We speak a lot about finding God. This is rubbish. We don't find God; he finds us! The story of the Bible is about a God who acts in human history, not a passive deity who plays a game of hide and seek. God seeks us out. His outstretched hand came to Adam in the Garden: "Where are you?" God came to the Hebrew people imprisoned in

Egypt and by the power of his outstretched hand led them to a land of freedom. Even though life tumbled in for the chosen people, the prophet announced, "God's hand is not shortened, that it cannot save."

God's hand is never longer than in Jesus Christ. In Jesus Christ God became man and shared fully in the contradictions of human existence. In the hands of Jesus we affirm that we see the hand of God at work. Look at those hands! Are they not beautiful—strong and firm, yet gentle? They are healing hands, bringing sight to the blind and health to the cripple. They are forgiving hands, a true embodiment of giving people another chance. They are loving hands, nailed to a cross in an ultimate act of self-giving. Jesus Christ is the way God has always dealt with his people.

PRAYER   *Almighty God, thou art our Creator, Sustainer, and Redeemer. Before we were formed thou didst know us and call us to be faithful sons. Thanks and praise be unto thee for the salvation which comes to us and all men in thine outstretched hand. Amen.*

EL SHADDAI

SCRIPTURE   When Abram was ninety-nine years old the Lord appeared to Abram, and said to him, "I am God Almighty; walk before me, and be blameless. And I will make my covenant between me and you, and will multiply you exceedingly." (Gen. 17:1-2.)

> For the Lord is a great God,
>   and a great King above all gods.
> In his hand are the depths of the earth;
>   the heights of the mountains are his
>   also. (Ps. 95:3-4.)

MEDITATION   A number of years ago J. B. Phillips wrote a book that caused a sensation by its startling title alone: *Your God Is Too Small*. The basic theme was that, although we are adults living in a world come of age, our idea of God has not grown beyond the kindergarten level of the church school. He mentioned that many of us think of God as a "resident policeman," "grand old man," "heavenly bosom," and other assorted images. Having too small an idea of God is nothing new, for this was a problem of people in Old Testament times, too. For example, some saw God as a local deity— the God of Bethel or the God of Jerusalem who was nowhere else to be found and worshiped. Others understood God to be a God of the Hebrew nation and not of the world—one

20

who led them to smashing victories over their enemies. Still others believed that God would be satisfied by elaborate sacrifices and would ignore the moral life of the worshiper. All these ideas of God were too small, as the prophets attempted to show. The people should have known better anyway! God had revealed himself to Abram as *El Shaddai,* which means "Almighty." Christian symbolism represents God's all-powerful nature by placing the Hebrew word for *El Shaddai* in a circle surrounded with rays of light, standing for divinity.

God is Almighty God! He is not a local deity. We do not have to journey to a particular shrine to find that God is near at hand, the very source of life itself. Nor is he a national God—a product of the U. S.A., or any other country. God does not exist for the nation's sake, but the nation exists for his sake. He is the God of the world and all men who dwell thereon. God is the God of all life. He is not simply the God of Sundays; he is the God of the whole week. Life cannot be neatly divided into sacred and secular, for God is active and alive everywhere. He calls man into complete service, and our worship in the sanctuary is in vain if we do not worship him in our work, in our play, in our homes, and in our communities.

The power of God is the power of love. Far too often we have considered God's power as wanton and destructive—a hurricane, an earthquake, or a tornado. But the Bible teaches us to understand God's power in terms of God's love. He deals with us sinners graciously, and we do not deserve it. We deserve death; he gives us life. We deserve defeat; he gives us victory. We deserve loneliness; he gives us fellowship. The power of love allows itself to appear to man in a form less than almighty, in the form of a lowly servant, and permits itself to be at the power of sinful man even to crucifixion. As we contemplate the event of Jesus Christ, we come to know that the true nature of God's power is suffering love. As Martin Luther put it, "In God's great hall and castle dwells only love."

PRAYER   *O Lord God, thy name is power and love. We confess that we are unable to find peace, joy, and hope unless thou dost give it to us. May thy name become more than a mere word; may it be a living reality in our lives. O God, be thou the sun around which our small worlds revolve, and the fire which warms our hearts. Let us sing praises unto thee and bless thy name forever. Amen.*

 YAHWEH

SCRIPTURE   Now Moses was keeping the flock of his father-in-law, Jethro, the priest of Midian; and he led his flock to the west side of the wilderness, and came to Horeb, the mountain of God. And the angel of the Lord appeared to him in a flame of fire out of the midst of a bush; and he looked, and lo, the bush was burning, yet it was not consumed. And Moses said, "I will turn aside and see this great sight, why the bush is not burnt." . . . God called to him out of the bush, "Moses, Moses!" And he said, "Here am I." . . .

Then Moses said to God, "If I come to the people of Israel and say to them, 'The God of your fathers has sent me to you,' and they ask me, 'What is his name?' what shall I say to them?" God said to Moses, "I AM WHO I AM." (Exod. 3:1-3, 4b, 13-14.)

MEDITATION   John Baillie wrote in *Our Knowledge of God:*

The witness of all true religion is that there is no reality which more directly confronts us than the reality of God. No other reality is nearer to us than He. The realities of sense are more obvious, but His is the more intimate, touching us as it does so much nearer to the core of our being.

God is the only reality which does not fade away and disappoint us. He is the one God, the only true God. He allows us to worship our idols, to bend our knees at pagan altars, and to drink at foreign springs, but he does not stop being our God and confronting us at the center of our lives.

The witness of the Bible is unanimous: God is with his people. The one God chooses one people, one history, one book, and one Christ to reveal himself to all nations. In the history of Israel, we find our history. In their encounter with God, we begin to understand how to speak of our meeting with him. God spoke to Moses out of a burning bush, which, although it burned, was not consumed. When God met Moses he made clear who he was: "I am who I am." This

23

phrase is actually a translation of the Hebrew word Yahweh, perhaps the most common name for God in the Old Testament. When written in Hebrew and surrounded by a circle it is a powerful symbol of God. It reminds us that as God came to Moses, laid a demand upon his life, and told him who he was, God comes to us in our day. His presence is not one which comes apart from all other presences, but one which comes through them. Indeed, he comes in the burning bushes which grow along our pathways.

God comes to us through the burning bush of nature. It is wrong to say that nature "proves" God, for it does not. Still God comes to us in the world which he has made, and we sense the majesty of God in nature. As the ancient psalmist said, "The heavens declare the glory of God; and the firmament showeth his handiwork" (19:1, K.J.V.).

God comes to us through the burning bush of a Christian home. When you ask a group of young people why they believe in God, they usually answer, "Because my parents do." Children sometimes adopt the beliefs of their parents without making them their own. This is a mistake, but at the same time, God does reach out through the loving arms of parents.

God comes to us through the burning bush of fellowship. We find God in the service of our fellows, not in isolation from them. The New Testament puts it quite plainly: He who does not love does not know God; however, if we love one another, God dwells in us. The face of God is in the face of the neighbor!

God comes to us in the burning bush of life. All our experience points to God, if we are receptive to his coming. God is life, and without him real life is impossible. He has not left himself without witnesses in any event, but reveals

24

himself in suffering and strength, in sorrow and joy, in poverty and prosperity. All our longing is basically longing for God. As Augustine said, "Our hearts are restless until they rest in thee."

PRAYER   *O God of the burning bush, thou dost speak to us in accents clear and strong. Thou art closer to us than our very breathing, nearer than hands and feet. Make us aware of thy holy presence so that all we do may be an offering unto thee. Give us ears to hear thy word, eyes to see thy glory, and hands to do thy work; through Jesus Christ our Lord. Amen.*

ALL-SEEING EYE

SCRIPTURE   For the word of God is living and active, sharper than any two-edged sword, piercing to the division of soul and spirit, of joints and marrow, and discerning the thoughts and intentions of the heart. And before him no creature is hidden, but all are open and laid bare to the eyes of him with whom we have to do. (Heb. 4:12-13.)

MEDITATION   We are creatures of the mask, rarely approaching one another in openness or honesty. Whenever

25

we are threatened with reality our defense mechanisms go to work quickly and throw up a protective wall around the little countries of our egos. Shakespeare's familiar words still ring true:

> All the world's a stage,
> And all the men and women merely players.

T. S. Eliot had our masks in mind when he wrote:

> We are the hollow men
> We are the stuffed men
> Leaning together
> Headpieces filled with straw. Alas!
> Our dried voices, when
> We whisper together
> Are quiet and meaningless
> As wind in dry grass
> Or rats' feet over broken glass
> In our dry cellar.

We are men in hiding; we hide from ourselves, from our neighbors, and from God. Our hiding from God is vain, however. Although we may quite successfully pass ourselves off as something we are not to ourselves and our neighbors, we cannot hide our true feelings from God. He is the all-seeing eye who pierces our defenses, lays bare our thoughts and motives, and strikes through to the innermost intimacies of our being. J. B. Phillips has made an arresting translation of Heb. 4:13: "No creature has any cover from the sight of God; everything lies naked and exposed before the eyes of him with whom we have to do."

Who of us does not want to escape that steady, piercing

gaze which calls us to question and melts our cherished idols? Yet we know that there is no escape from confronting the living God, for he is the source of all life. The writer of Ps. 139 realized the folly of trying to escape God. If he ascended into heaven, God was there. If he went to the land of the dead, God was there too. He could flee to the uttermost parts of the sea and take refuge in the darkness of the night, but God would still pursue him. Yes, he is the God "with whom we have to do."

God comes to us in judgment because he is perfect love. Never once in the Bible is his judgment considered apart from his love, but rather it comes as a natural result of his love. God is not a tyrant or a celestial policeman who tracks us down to punish us, but a God of sacrificial love whose will is for us to have abundant life. Because he wills the health of his creatures, he cannot tolerate the sin which destroys them. The psalmist realized that God is love, so he did not stop with confessing his desire to flee from God. He went on to praise God and call his name wonderful and concluded by asking God to change his life:

> Search me, O God, and know my heart!
> Try me and know my thoughts!
> And see if there be any wicked way in me,
> and lead me in the way everlasting!
> (Ps. 139:23-24.)

PRAYER   *Almighty God, unto whom all hearts are open, all desires known, and from whom no secrets are hid; cleanse the thoughts of our hearts by the inspiration of thy Holy Spirit, that we may perfectly love thee, and worthily magnify thy holy name; through Christ our Lord. Amen.*

II

MEDITATIONS ON SYMBOLS
OF GOD THE SON

CROWN

SCRIPTURE   Now when Jesus was born in Bethlehem of Judea in the days of Herod the king, behold, wise men from the East came to Jerusalem, saying, "Where is he who has been born King of the Jews?" (Matt. 2:1-2a.)

Pilate said to him, "So you are a king?" Jesus answered, "You say that I am a king. For this I was born, and for this I have come into the world, to bear witness to the truth." (John 18:37.)

Jesus of Nazareth, the King of the Jews. (John 19:19.)

For he is Lord of lords and King of kings. . . . (Rev. 17:14b.)

MEDITATION   Jesus Christ is King. The Scripture passages quoted above are taken from widely separated places in the story of Jesus, but all make a single affirmation: Jesus Christ is King! He was King at his birth as wise men from the East came to pay him homage with their gifts of gold, frankincense, and myrrh. He was King at his trial when he stood in quiet dignity, his very silence shaking imperial Rome to its foundations. He was King at his death, in a way which those who

31

wrote the cynical inscription that hung over his head could never imagine. He is King in his resurrection and glory, as the church confesses: "Lord of lords and King of kings!" Christian art represents his kingship by a crown.

To say that Jesus Christ is King of kings is to indicate that he has authority. Jesus spoke with authority, and not as the scribes. There is a great difference between speaking from authorities, speaking as an authority, and speaking as *the* authority. The man who speaks from authorities without adding his own insights speaks as one who has no experience; the one who speaks as an authority speaks as one who has been encountered; and the one who speaks as *the* authority speaks as one in whom the revelation of God comes decisively. Only one man has ever spoken as *the* authority. Men who gathered about Jesus sensed this kingly quality.

Again, to say that Jesus is King of kings means that he is *my* authority. When we make this affirmation it is not an objective description of fact that is true for someone else, but not for us. As Americans, we may say that Gustaf VI is the King of Sweden. Of course, since we are Americans, he is not our king. But when we say that Jesus Christ is King we affirm that he is our King and we are his subjects. As King of our lives, he is our judge and our redeemer. Our total and ultimate loyalty is sworn to him as to no one else, or he cannot be our King.

To say that Jesus is King of kings means a third thing: He holds authority for all. His authority is not limited to only one area—the spiritual—but includes the whole of life. His truth does not accommodate our tastes; it is his truth, whether we like it or not. His truth is not merely for some men;

it is for all men, rich and poor, humble and proud, black and white.

Once the great warrior king of Sweden, Charles XII, paid a surprise visit to a church in Ystad, Sweden. Overwhelmed by the royal hero's presence, the pastor laid aside his text and substituted a glowing eulogy of the king and the royal family. Some months later the church received a gift from King Charles. It was a crucifix. Charles had enclosed these instructions: "This is to hang on the pillar opposite the pulpit, so that all who shall stand there will be reminded of their proper subject." This was in 1716. The crucifix hangs there to this very day, life-size and lifelike, with human hair matted under the crown of actual thorns. Charles showed himself to be a true king, for he recognized that his only authority came from Christ, the King.

PRAYER *O King of men, Master of our lives, entering into the glory by the cross, to whom all authority is given, both in heaven and on earth, we acknowledge thy sovereignty over every realm of life. Come, O Lord, enter into thy kingdom; subdue the world by the might of thy love. Subdue us by the might of thy love, and grant that our faithful actions will extend thy kingship over all the world until thou dost come again in triumph. Amen.*

CANDLE

SCRIPTURE   In him was life, and the life was the light of men. The light shines in the darkness, and the darkness has not overcome it. (John 1:4-5.)

Again Jesus spoke to them, saying, "I am the light of the world; he who follows me will not walk in darkness, but will have the light of life." (John 8:12.)

MEDITATION   A candle refers to Jesus as the light of the world. Upon the altars of many churches you will find two candles, symbolizing our Lord's twofold nature—human and divine. These candles are lit during the service of worship, and they proclaim to all who see them that Jesus Christ is the light of the world. In early centuries of the Christian Church the candles on the altar served a more functional purpose; they gave light for the minister of the congregation to read by. Services were often held at night—or in dark catacombs—and some sort of light was needed in order to read.

Throughout the Bible light is compared with darkness. It is an interesting figure of speech and has several different meanings. In the Old Testament light and darkness were sometimes used to contrast prosperity and happiness with adversity and sorrow. In New Testament times everything associated with God was light, while the powers of evil were characterized by darkness. When I John wrote, "God is light and in him is no darkness at all," he was saying that God

34

is wholly good, and there is no evil in his nature. I John also speaks about the necessity of walking in the light, and not in darkness, if we are to have fellowship with God.

When Jesus said that he was the light of the world he said at least two things about himself. He was saying, "Fellowship with me means happiness, not sorrow." Happiness is of the light, sorrow is of the darkness. Jesus was certainly not suggesting that Christians would not know sorrow. The Man of the cross knew better than this and was frank to say, "In the world you have tribulation." This sorrow, however, is transitory and defeated already by the power of God. So, Jesus added immediately, "Cheer up! I have overcome the world." In fellowship with Jesus was perfect joy—deep, abiding, and real beyond all reality. The early Christians were joyful Christians who lived in praise and thanksgiving that their sins had been forgiven through Jesus Christ.

It is indeed ironic that modern day Christians should often display attitudes that makes those who look for joy turn away from the church to continue their lonely search. Algernon Charles Swinburne probably wrote "Thou hast conquered, O pale Galilean; the world has grown gray from thy breath"; after being in the fellowship of a certain kind of "religious" people. He certainly did not get such an idea after reading the Gospel accounts of Jesus' life, for Jesus saw joy as one of the fruits of faith.

Jesus was also saying, "I am wholly good, and there is no evil in me." This was another way of announcing that he was the Messiah, who participated perfectly in God's action and purposes. As wholly good, Jesus Christ set his face against evil wherever he found it—whether it was in the street or the synagogue, among rich or poor. How did he choose to overcome evil? Not by force of arms, as the Zealots expected him to do, but rather by the force of sacrificial love which reached its climax on the cross. In that moment evil was defeated, and although evil is still with us, we fight it as an enemy whose final doom has already been sealed by the life, death, and resurrection of Jesus Christ, our light and life.

PRAYER   *Almighty and merciful God, thou art light, and in thee is no darkness at all. Drive out the darkness of our souls, deliver us from temptation and evil, set our feet in the path of light. Give us the ancient knowledge that it is better to light a candle than to curse the darkness. And as we have received light from thee, may we spread that light unto all the world; through Jesus Christ. Amen.*

FISH

SCRIPTURE   Blessed are you when men revile you and persecute you and utter all kinds of evil against you falsely on my account. Rejoice and be glad, for your reward is great in heaven, for so men persecuted the prophets who were before you. (Matt. 5:11-12.)

Beloved, do not be surprised at the fiery ordeal which comes upon you to prove you, as though something strange were happening to you. But rejoice in so far as you share Christ's sufferings, that you may also rejoice and be glad when his glory is revealed. If you are reproached for the name of Christ, you are blessed, because the spirit of glory and of God rests upon you. . . . Therefore let those who suffer according to God's will do right and entrust their souls to a faithful creator. (I Pet. 4:12-14, 19.)

MEDITATION   A young Greek slave was on an errand in the home of his master's friend in the city of Rome. He gave his message to the mistress of the house, who was seated with her maidens in the court. As he turned to leave he caught the eye of one of the slave girls, a Greek like himself, and said, *"Ichthus?"* She flushed, clasped her hands, and said with a glad smile, *"Ichthus!"* The mistress saw, heard, and frowningly bade the girl to go on with her embroidery. But she thought to herself, "What could that word mean that it could bring that happy smile?" On her husband's return she asked him what *Ichthus* meant.

"It means 'fish,' my dear," he responded.

More puzzled than ever, she said to her maid, "What does *Ichthus* mean?"

"Madam, it means 'fish,'" replied the maid.

To the mistress all the word meant was "fish," but to these two young people, strangers and slaves, it meant "We're both Christians. This is our password. We both love our Lord Jesus Christ."

Except for the cross, the fish is regarded as the oldest Christian symbol. It was used by persecuted Christians as a code name for Christ in order to avoid arrest and execution by

37

Roman authorities. When a picture of a fish appeared outside a Christian home it meant that the Lord's Supper would be observed that night, under cover. In the Roman catacombs the fish was carved on the slabs of marble or stone which sealed the remains of Christians. Why did the early Christians use a fish to represent Christ? The first letters of the Greek acrostic phrase meaning "Jesus Christ, Son of God, Savior" spelled out the word for fish, *Ichthus*.

Today, the fish calls Christians to remember the sufferings of our Lord and of his church. We must never forget that the demands of the gospel are set over against the expectations of the world and to follow the gospel often means rejection, persecution, and death. This is as true in the twentieth century as it was in the first. Many Christians died in Nazi concentration camps, and the faith is still persecuted in Communist states.

The fish also makes another, more challenging call: Remember that all Christians must be ready to be persecuted and to suffer death for their faith. Although democratic states do not persecute the Christian faith, those who live in democracies often find themselves rejected by their neighbors for trying to follow what they believe to be Christian principles. With the witness of Jesus Christ and the martyrs of the church ever before us, we should bear our persecution with courage, hope, forgiveness, and thanksgiving.

PRAYER   *Almighty God, we confess that we are reluctant to make the needed sacrifices for the proclamation of the gospel. We have been silent when we should have spoken, and we have spoken when we should have been silent. We have desired safety more than salvation, comfort more than courage, peace more than glory. Grant us, we beseech thee, a new vision of the church as the body of Christ which challenges us anew to dedicate ourselves wholly to thee. Fill us with the conviction that it is far better to die for the truth than to live for a lie. Amen.*

CHI RHO

SCRIPTURE   Who shall separate us from the love of Christ? Shall tribulation, or distress, or persecution, or famine, or nakedness, or peril, or sword? . . . No, in all these things we are more than conquerors through him who loved us. For I am sure that neither death, nor life, nor angels, nor principalities, nor things present, nor things to come, nor powers, nor height, nor depth, nor anything else in all creation, will be able to separate us from the love of God in Christ Jesus our Lord. (Rom. 8:35, 37-39.)

MEDITATION   The setting sun cast weird shadows across the rough landscape. Soldiers, tattered and tired from many battles, settled down to sleep. Guards leaned heavily upon their spears, peering out into the gathering darkness.

Constantine the Great looked into the swift-flowing, yellow waters of the Tiber. He thought of the next days, when the waters would be mixed with the blood of Roman soldiers—perhaps even his own blood. His forces hardly seemed adequate for the great battle with Emperor Maxentius. Constantine's mind raced back to the events of that afternoon. He saw—from the very spot on which he now stood—a bright cross. On it were the words *In hoc signo vinces,* "in this sign conquer." What did the strange vision mean? Constantine lay down on his cloak and fell into a troubled sleep. In a dream the great soldier was confronted with the Christ.

When he awoke, Constantine knew that the sign in the sky stood for Christ. He ordered his men to paint the symbol on their standards and shields before going into battle. With the cross as their sign, they drove the enemy into the Tiber, and the pagan Maxentius was drowned. Constantine was hailed as sole ruler of the western empire. In A.D. 313 he issued the Edict of Milan, which guaranteed Christians freedom to practice their religion, and later he convened the famous Nicene Council.

The sign under which Constantine marched to victory is known as the *Chi Rho,* which is the way we say X and P in Greek. These are the first two letters of the Greek word which means Christ and are found in woodcarvings and in the stained-glass windows of many churches.

Whether this story of Constantine's vision belongs to history or legend is really unimportant. What matters is that we believe that by this sign we conquer. In Jesus Christ we find what was always and is forever true: God comes to defeated man and gives him the victory. Nothing—absolutely nothing—separates us from the love of God. Tribulation, distress, persecution, famine, nakedness, peril, death—these are all dark realities of our torn world. Yet the greatest reality is God's love, which is always meeting us at the point of deepest need.

What battles are you fighting now? Is it a battle with the temptation to be more "practical" and abandon your ideals? Is it a battle with doubt which threatens to drive you to despair? Is it a battle with fear which cripples your creative capacity? Whatever the battle, it is not too much for God. We are more than conquerors through him who loved us. Charles Wesley wrote:

> Soldiers of Christ, arise,
> And put your armor on,
> Strong in the strength which God supplies
> Through His eternal Son.

PRAYER   *O God, thou hast spoken thine everlasting "Yes" in the midst of all the negations of life. Nothing has power over thee, but thou hast power over all. We thank thee for thy love which has been with us all the days of our lives and which is faithful even in our dying. We thank thee for all events which call us to explore deeper resources of faith and to learn of thy son, Jesus Christ our Lord. Amen.*

41

THE GOOD SHEPHERD

SCRIPTURE   "Truly, truly, I say unto you, I am the door of the sheep. All who came before me are thieves and robbers; but the sheep did not heed them. I am the door; if any one enters by me, he will be saved, and will go in and out and find pasture. . . . I am the good shepherd. The good shepherd lays down his life for the sheep. He who is a hireling and not a shepherd, whose own the sheep are not, sees the wolf coming and leaves the sheep and flees; and the wolf snatches them and scatters them. He flees because he is a hireling and cares nothing for the sheep. I am the good shepherd; I know my own and my own know me . . . and I lay down my life for the sheep." (John 10:7-9, 11-14.)

MEDITATION   We must understand the claim of Jesus to be the good shepherd against the religious background of the Hebrew people. Some eighty times the Old Testament writers compare the people to sheep and God to a shepherd. Perhaps the most loved psalm of all, the famous Ps. 23, pictures God as our shepherd. When Jesus announced that he was the good shepherd he was again making the astounding claim to be the one whom God had sent to redeem his people. What does the good shepherd do for his sheep?

First of all, he leads the sheep. Unlike western shepherds, the eastern shepherd did not follow his sheep. He led them "beside still waters." So it is with Jesus. He is ahead of us, and all our human history moves toward its realization in him. Many times we have our doubts and believe that Jesus is somehow a "back number" and that Christian discipleship is hopelessly behind our enlightened times—"prescientific." In such times of doubt let us remember the indelible mark this One has left on history—the One who came not with armies and swords, but with love and forgiveness. All the armies of persecution have not been able to erase his name; the centuries have not been able to dull his living presence; and no one else has so embodied message and person in one perfect whole. H. G. Wells wrote, "He is too much for our small hearts."

Secondly, he protects the sheep. Ps. 23 indicates the shepherd's instruments of protection as rod and staff. With his rod he prodded the sheep into the stone-walled fold time and again at nightfall. With his hook staff he lifted the small ones over perilous stones. The good shepherd is not a hireling. He does not flee when the wolf comes to prey on the flock, but will lay down his life for the sheep. So Christ saw his mission in terms of dying on a cross for the sake of his sheep. The sheep are protected from sin and death by their dying and rising Lord. They are ushered into a new relationship so that their cups run over and that the banquet tables of life are full with all the needful food.

Finally, he keeps the flock together. The good shepherd cares for each of the flock as if there were but one sheep to care for. When a careful count shows that one is missing he will search for the sheep until he finds it, and then he will rejoice greatly, calling his neighbors together, and saying, "Rejoice with me, for I have found my sheep which was lost" (Luke 15:6). This has special significance for the church.

There is much in these days that would scatter us—doctrinal division, socioeconomic differences, individual pettiness. Yet, through his Holy Spirit, the good shepherd will keep the flock of his church together as witnesses to his faithfulness, and he will add to the flock daily.

PRAYER   *Almighty and most merciful Father; We have erred, and strayed from thy ways like lost sheep. We have followed too much the devices and desires of our own hearts. We have offended against thy holy laws. We have left undone those things which we ought to have done; And we have done those things which we ought not to have done; And there is no health in us. But thou, O Lord, have mercy upon us, miserable offenders. Spare thou those, O God, who confess their faults. Restore thou those who are penitent; According to thy promises declared unto mankind in Christ Jesus our Lord. And grant, O most merciful Father, for his sake; that we may hereafter live a godly, righteous, and sober life, to the glory of thy holy Name. Amen.*

AGNUS DEI

SCRIPTURE   He was oppressed, and he was afflicted,
    yet he opened not his mouth;
  like a lamb that is led to the slaughter,
    and like a sheep that before its shearers
    is dumb,
    so he opened not his mouth. (Is. 53:7.)

While we were yet helpless, at the right time Christ died for the ungodly. Why, one will hardly die for a righteous man—though perhaps for a good man one will dare even to die. But God shows his love for us in that while we were yet sinners, Christ died for us. (Rom. 5:6.)

The Lamb that was slain. (Rev. 13:8.)

MEDITATION   Christ, who has been pictured as the good shepherd, is also portrayed in Christian art as the lamb of God. One of the earliest symbols, it was frequently used in the Roman catacombs in at least two poses. Sometimes the lamb is lying on a book of seven seals, and sometimes the lamb is standing with a banner of triumph, symbolizing resurrection.

To understand why this symbol is perhaps the most meaningful of all used to describe Christ's work we must remember that in Old Testament times a guilt offering of a lamb was made to God in order to cleanse oneself of sin. In the death of Jesus Christ the church announces that God has acted on

45

man's behalf in a decisive way. Jesus is the lamb of God that takes away the sins of the world. He is, at the same time, the offering and the one who offers up.

The *Agnus Dei* symbolizes that forgiveness is infinitely costly to God. We often forget that although forgiveness doesn't cost us anything, it costs God everything. God's forgiveness has been taken too lightly, and many believe that it is an easy routine—that God passes lightly over our sins like an indulgent grandfather. The most familiar expression of this attitude comes from the German poet Heine, who said: "God will forgive us: that is His business." This is not the case, however. Surely the nature of God is love and forgiveness, but it is not an easy indulgence. His love and forgiveness comes as one who has borne our sins and who knows the pain of crucifixion. So great is God's love for us that he gave up his only son as a means of dealing with our sins.

The *Agnus Dei* cannot be confined to any one moment of time. The cross is contemporary as Christ is contemporary. In George Bernard Shaw's play *Saint Joan* Cauchon asks, "Must then a Christ perish in torment in every age to save those that have no imagination?" In a real sense, Christ does perish in every generation to save us. Some years after the crucifixion, the author of the epistle to the Hebrews wrote that some "crucify to themselves the Son of God afresh, and put him to open shame," (6:6, K.J.V.) bearing out the contention that Christ still suffers at the hands of sinful men even though the historical crucifixion is finished. The greatest agony which Christ experienced on Calvary—his heart breaking over the sins of man—is a continuous agony as he beholds our sin. "Behold, the lamb of God, who takes away the sins of the world!" Behold him now.

PRAYER   *Almighty God, who of thine infinite compassion dost forgive us and restore us to a right relationship with thee, we confess that we have found it easy to sin and easy to ask forgiveness. Help us to understand that our sin serves to crucify Jesus Christ afresh and that our repentance must be sincere. As we stand at the foot of the cross, may we not turn away, but rather accept the love which comes from thee. Lord, have mercy upon us. Christ, have mercy upon us. Lord, have mercy upon us. Amen.*

ALPHA AND OMEGA

SCRIPTURE   And he who sat upon the throne said, "Behold, I make all things new." Also he said, "Write this, for these words are trustworthy and true." And he said to me, "It is done! I am the Alpha and the Omega, the beginning and the end. To the thirsty I will give water without price from the fountain of the water of life." (Rev. 21:5-7.)

MEDITATION   Alpha and Omega are the first and last letters in the Greek alphabet. They stand for the beginning and the end, the first and the last. They are used as a monogram to indicate that Jesus Christ is an eternal figure, not limited

47

to a particular time or place. The text from Revelation might be translated, "I am the A and the Z."

"I am the A." Christ was represented by John as being present with the Creator God at the beginning—at the "laying of the foundations of the world." Not only is this true for the book of Revelation, but also for the Gospel written by John. The Gospel begins with a climax, crashing words which tumble like a giant waterfall, parallel to the beginning of the first creation story in Genesis. "In the beginning was the Word, and the Word was with God, and the Word was God. He was in the beginning with God; all things were made through him, and without him was not anything made that was made." (John 1:1-3.) John was saying that from the very beginning—yes, even the twilight time and darkness before the Creator formed the world—God was the creative, active, seeking God whose very nature was to come to man in Jesus of Nazareth.

"I am the Z." Jesus Christ—the same man who lived, died, and was buried—will also be present at the last. He will bring all his enemies under his feet, and to him will belong the final victory. Christians believe that all history is God's history, and it is moving toward a God-appointed purpose. To be sure, this is an affirmation of faith, not of fact, for much of life is meaningless, and our history seems to be "moving progressively backward." Yet God is faithful even in situations which we cannot understand. Jesus Christ is the Z. He will not leave his work of love incomplete; good will have the final word over evil; and his kingdom will be forever, world without end. This is the faith which we need for days in which man is dying of despair even more than he is of physical hunger.

48

Jesus Christ is the A and Z of history, but he is also the A and Z of your life. Life begins when we understand that Jesus Christ gives us meaning, and we are dead until we know him. "To the thirsty I will give water without price from the fountain of the water of life." Remember when Jesus spoke to an outcast Samaritan woman at a lonely well? She was drawing cool water from the well, and he offered her water of another kind—a vital relationship with him. She ran into the city, telling everyone, "Come, see a man who told me all that I ever did" (John 4:29). Jesus Christ tells us everything we ever did, which is to say that he shows us who we are and who we can become. He is the mirror of life, and as we fix our gaze on him, we find our own images reflected in an entirely new way. "Behold, I make all things new." Even our old, tattered, inadequate, false, dead selves! He does this—he can do this—because he is the Alpha and the Omega.

PRAYER *O Thou who art from everlasting to everlasting, without beginning or end of days, hear our prayer as we draw close to thee. Quench our thirst, which remains despite all earthly springs, and satisfy our hunger. Help us not to fear life, but to embrace it as a glorious gift from thy hand. Make us men of faith who are able to walk freely across the anxious and uncertain waters of life, looking to Jesus, the author and finisher of our faith, the Alpha and the Omega of our history. Amen.*

49

III

MEDITATIONS ON SYMBOLS
OF GOD THE HOLY SPIRIT
AND OF THE TRINITY

III

MEDITATIONS ⚬ SYMBOLS
OF GOD THE HOLY SPIRIT
AND OF THE TRINITY

DESCENDING DOVE

SCRIPTURE   Then Jesus came from Galilee to the Jordan to John, to be baptized by him. John would have prevented him, saying, "I need to be baptized by you, and do you come to me?" But Jesus answered him, "Let it be so now; for thus it is fitting for us to fulfil all righteousness." Then he consented. And when Jesus was baptized, he went up immediately from the water, and behold, the heavens were opened and he saw the Spirit of God descending like a dove, and alighting on him; and lo, a voice from heaven, saying, "This is my beloved Son, with whom I am well pleased." (Matt. 3:13-17.)

MEDITATION   The first three Gospels record the baptism of Jesus, describing the Holy Spirit descending like a dove. Because of this the most familiar symbol for the Holy Spirit is a descending dove. This powerful symbol helps us to understand the nature of God the Holy Spirit.

The dove flies freely through the air with a beautiful gracefulness. The free flight of a dove is suggestive of the freedom of the Holy Spirit. John spoke of this freedom when he wrote: "The wind blows where it wills, and you hear the sound of

53

it, but you do not know whence it comes or whither it goes; so it is with every one who is born of the Spirit." (John 3:8.) The Holy Spirit is like a dove; he is like the wind. Man cannot control the Holy Spirit and use him for his own purposes. The Holy Spirit works as God wills. As the Spirit is free so are those who are born of the Spirit. They have the graceful nature of the dove, and although they are not immune to suffering, sin, disappointment, and death, they are free from their crippling blows. The Apostle Paul is the best example of the Spirit giving a man strength. He was run out of the city, stoned, jeered, shipwrecked, hungry, thirsty, a prisoner, but in all of this tragedy, he was able to say, "Thanks be to God through Jesus Christ our Lord!" God's sustaining Spirit gave him the victory.

The dove which symbolizes the Holy Spirit is descending. The Christian story is not about a God who must be searched out by the efforts of man's mind and his science, but a God who is active in our history. The Old Testament is filled with stories about God coming to man and calling him. This was the experience of Abraham, Moses, Isaiah, Jeremiah, and all the other heroes of the faith. God's visiting his people reached a climax in the life, death, and resurrection of Jesus Christ. In Jesus Christ man was brought face to face with the tremendous fact that God cared for man more than man cared for himself, and he sealed his promises with the blood of his Son. But the early church went beyond the crucifixion of Jesus. The experience of the followers of Jesus affirmed that nothing on earth could frustrate God's power in Jesus Christ and that although Jesus was truly dead, he was now truly alive. God did not stop visiting his people with Jesus Christ, but through the Holy Spirit, visits his people always.

This is both a comfort and a challenge; comforting, because God is love and sustains his people in their trials and darkness; challenging, because the Spirit calls us to abandon walking in darkness and to begin walking in light. Will you take this comfort and challenge to yourself?

PRAYER   *O Thou who dost come to us as Holy Spirit, we make our humble confession: We have sought to control thee, instead of asking thee to direct us in all our doings; we have attempted to justify ourselves by works, instead of accepting thy justification of us in faith. Forgive us for our dead spirit and rekindle the flames of Pentecost in our lives. Help us to listen to thee when thou dost speak, and to trust thee when thou art silent. Pour out on us and thy whole church thy Holy Spirit so that thy kingdom might come and thy will might be done on earth, as it is in heaven; in the name of Jesus Christ we pray. Amen.*

SEVEN-TONGUED FLAME

SCRIPTURE   When the day of Pentecost had come, they were all together in one place. And suddenly a sound came from heaven like the rush of a mighty wind, and it filled all the house where they were sitting. And there appeared to them tongues of fire, distributed and resting on each one of them. And they were all filled with the Holy Spirit and began to speak in other tongues, as the Spirit gave them utterance. . . . And all were amazed and perplexed, saying to one another, "What does this mean?" But others mocking said, "They are filled with new wine." (Acts 2:1-4, 12-13.)

MEDITATION   Gathered at Pentecost for worship, the apostles had such an overwhelming experience that they became rowdy—a far cry from some of our lifeless church meetings today! A crowd soon gathered to watch the proceedings and was sharply divided in its feeling. Some people were willing to be open-minded and asked, "What does this mean?" Others wrote the apostles off as being intoxicated. "They are filled with new wine" was the opinion. The reality of the matter was that the apostles were drunk on the new wine of the Spirit. God—the same God who came in Jesus Christ —had come again into their midst, giving assurance that he was ever present with them in the power of his Holy Spirit.

A popular symbol for the Holy Spirit is the seven-tongued flame because Luke, in recounting the story of Pentecost, said that the apostles' experience with God came like tongues of fire, resting upon their heads and giving them utterance. As a result of this visitation of the Spirit the apostles began to speak in other tongues, and the church received a new birth of power.

The seven-tongued flame signifies that no man speaks the truth of God unless God himself gives him utterance. When the early church proclaimed the gospel message the bearers of the good news were not spinning neat systems of thought about God; they were announcing events. They were not spouting views; they were giving news. The gospel which they proclaimed was not their gospel; it was known as God's gospel or the gospel of Jesus Christ. That message which turned the world upside down and set cold hearts aflame came from God. It transformed the believer's life through the ministry of the Holy Spirit. Certainly God used human messengers and laid a solemn charge on their lives, but in the end to him alone belonged the glory. As Paul said concerning the work at Corinth, "I planted, Apollos watered, but God gave the growth (I Cor. 3:6).

The seven-tongued flame signifies that God never stops confronting us with himself. God did not stop giving himself to Israel, but came in Jesus Christ. He continues giving himself today in the Holy Spirit. Christians believe that the Holy Spirit is the sustainer, the one who holds us together in the present tense. The Holy Spirit is the sustainer of our personal lives, giving us the courage to be. He is also the sustainer of our life together—in our homes, in our work, in our churches. Nietzsche cried, "God is dead!" But he was wrong. God is not dead. He is active and alive, coming to us in our space age as strongly as he ever came to man. When life is lived in obedient response to him man learns what it means to be full and free.

PRAYER   *Eternal God, send thy Holy Spirit into our lives, so that we may be directed according to thy will, defended from evil, protected from error, led into all truth and enriched in grace. Bear witness to our spirits that we are children of thine. Help us to realize that when thy Spirit is present in our lives there is liberty; through Jesus Christ our Lord. Amen.*

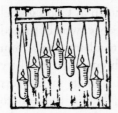

SEVEN LAMPS

SCRIPTURE   And the Spirit of the Lord shall rest upon him,
the spirit of wisdom and understanding,
the spirit of counsel and might,
the spirit of knowledge and the fear of the
Lord. (Isa. 11:2.)

And out of the throne proceeded lightnings and thunderings and voices: and there were seven lamps of fire burning before the throne, which are the seven Spirits of God. (Rev. 4:5, K.J.V.)

MEDITATION   A wealth of meaning is found in the seven lamps. The lamps include the three persons of the Trinity, representing heaven, and the four directions—north, south, east, and west—standing for earth. Each candle points to a gift of the Holy Spirit—wisdom, understanding, counsel, might, knowledge, true godliness, and the fear of the Lord.

These gifts of the Holy Spirit are active in character. You can count on that! The Spirit makes us creative persons who are always growing, always going on voyages of discovery. Far too many Christians have been content to imitate the idle servant in Jesus' parable who, out of timidity and fear, hid his master's talent in the ground. This was certainly not what the master had intended, as the parable made plain. He wanted the servant to grasp the opportunity to produce.

Christians must not be merely good. How faithless and pharisaical! Christians must be good for something.

It is urgent that we open ourselves to the creative work of the Spirit. Perhaps this is the only real issue facing us—whether we are open to creativity or closed, whether we are builders or wreckers. H. Richard Niebuhr wrote a few years before he died, "Nothing very important for mankind will happen as the result of our 'conquest' of space or as a result of the cessation of the cold war unless the human spirit is revived from within."

Another thing—the gifts of the Spirit are just that—gifts. As at Christmas some naughty children receive gifts which they do not deserve, so through his Holy Spirit God gives us gifts which no one merits. To say that a man is gifted is no compliment to the man, but a recognition of God's graciousness. The Christian life is properly one of thanksgiving and praise to God for his gifts, so freely given and so universally undeserved.

Finally, we have a solemn responsibility for these gifts. God's Spirit acts in no man who refuses fellowship with him. We are baptized into the church "free of charge" so to speak, but there comes a time when we are called on to appropriate our baptism with the response of faith. So it is with God's gifts, which were given us independent of our character. There comes a time when we must respond with faith for these gifts to be fully realized. Paul wrote to Timothy, "Stir up the gift of God, which is in thee." (II Tim. 1:6, K.J.V.)

Stir up the gift of God within you! Open yourself to the Spirit moving in the world and in your life. Deny yourself the luxury of routine living. Cultivate positive goodness—being good for something. Let your choking moralisms die. Care more for God than you do for life itself.

Isaac Watts wrote:

> Come, Holy Spirit, heavenly Dove,
> With all Thy quickening powers;
> Come, shed abroad a Saviour's love,
> And that shall kindle ours.

PRAYER   *O God, we dare pray to thee for a mighty rebirth in our lives. Stab us awake! Call us to creativity! Renew our sense of responsibility! Grant that we may show forth the fruits of thy Spirit to all men, and that whatever we do may point to thee and thy kingdom; through Jesus Christ, thy Creative Word. Amen.*

TRINITY SYMBOLS

SCRIPTURE   In the beginning God created the heavens and the earth. (Gen. 1:1.)

In the beginning was the Word, and the Word was with God, and the Word was God. (John 1:1.)

Nevertheless I tell you the truth: it is to your advantage that I go away, for if I do not go away, the Counselor will not come to you; but if I go, I will send him to you. (John 16:7.)

The grace of the Lord Jesus Christ and the love of God and the fellowship of the Holy Spirit be with you all. (II Cor. 13:14.)

MEDITATION   Christians do not worship three Gods— Father, Son, and Holy Spirit—we worship one God who has revealed himself to us in three ways. There is no competition between the persons of the Trinity; they exist in perfect harmony. All the symbols for the Trinity point to this truth.

61

Perhaps the most common Trinity symbol is an equilateral triangle. All the three persons of the Trinity are separate, as the sides of the triangle, yet all are joined like the triangle. All three sides are of equal length, reminding us that the three persons of the Trinity form the perfect unity of the Godhead.

Another symbol for the Trinity is three interwoven circles of equal size, symbolizing the unity, equality, and eternity of the three persons of the Trinity.

The fish, an early symbol for Jesus Christ, is also used to denote the Trinity. When used as a Trinity symbol, three fish are arranged in triangular form.

A symbol which we find in several different places and often associate with the French nation is the fleur-de-lis. It means "flower of the lily" and stands for the Trinity because of its threefold division. Although an early symbol, it does not express the equality of the persons of the Trinity since all three persons of the Godhead are not shown to be equal.

The story of the shamrock as a Trinity symbol is especially interesting. According to legend, Saint Patrick confronted the pagan king of Ireland and spoke to him about the Trinity. The king could not understand how three persons could be in one. Saint Patrick, being a resourceful preacher, picked a shamrock that was growing near and showed it to the king. "Is there one leaf or three?" he asked. The king confessed that he could not answer the question about the shamrock. Then Saint Patrick said that if he could not understand the mystery of the shamrock, there was no hope of his understanding such a deep mystery as the Holy Trinity.

As we face the question of life we encounter many deep mysteries. Among them is the mystery of God. We do not know all about him. Like Moses, we have only seen his back. We must confess that our sin has hidden the fullness of his revelation from our eyes. Like Paul, we see through a dark glass. But this does not lessen his demand upon our lives to be obedient to what we do know about him. Although we cannot understand, we must adore; although we cannot see clearly, we must follow.

PRAYER   *O eternal God, Father, Son, and Holy Spirit, grant that in the majesty of all creation we may behold thy power that upholds us, in the face of Jesus Christ thy love that seeks and saves us, and in new life within our souls thy Spirit kindling in us; that so even to our littleness thine infinite wonder may be revealed, O blessed Triune God. Amen.*

IV

MEDITATIONS ON SYMBOLS
OF HOLY WEEK

PALM LEAVES

SCRIPTURE   And they brought the colt to Jesus, and threw their garments on it; and he sat upon it. And many spread their garments on the road, and others spread leafy branches which they had cut from the fields. And those who went before and those who followed cried out, "Hosanna! Blessed be he who comes in the name of the Lord! Blessed be the kingdom of our father David that is coming! Hosanna in the highest!" (Mark 11:7-10.)

MEDITATION   Jesus realized the symbolic character of the universe. Men are moved by words, but he knew that they are grasped even more by silent dramatic gestures. Jesus could have stood in the streets of Jerusalem and shouted, "Your Messiah has come!" Instead, he chose to dramatically portray his messiahship by riding into the city upon an ass. He entered the city silently. He did not have to speak. The fact that he rode upon an ass spoke to the people with a symbol "too deep for words." He had drawn upon Israel's past history —which was always very closely present to the Hebrews— fulfilling Zechariah's prophecy that the Messiah would come riding on an ass. In this act Jesus announced once again that the kingdom of God was at hand and people were called on to repent and to believe his gospel.

Palm leaves symbolize the triumphal entry to Jesus into Jerusalem, the climax of what Edgar Goodspeed has called "The Great Offensive." In the Gospel stories, palm leaves were actually the silent symbols of response from the crowd to Jesus' dramatic announcement. They shouted, "Hosanna! Blessed be he who comes in the name of the Lord! . . . Hosanna in the highest!" And the palm leaves which they waved and threw in front of the triumphal procession indicated their excited devotion.

Palm leaves are necessary equipment for Christians today as we once again await his triumphal entry.

First, we need the palm leaf of penitence. We who wait know that we are not worthy of him who came and who is coming again. In the season of Lent, observed by many churches, Christians are asked to adopt a mood of genuine self-examination and penitence. Remembering the events of Holy Week, climaxing with Jesus' crucifixion, we must respond in penitence. Although those who shouted "Hosanna in the highest!" and those who crucified him were probably not the same crowd, within the hearts of those who shouted praise existed the same capacity for putting Jesus to death. And in the twisted, distorted faces around the cross we see our faces. "The remembrance of our sins is grievous unto us." Deep inside us we know that we are the ones who shout praise and the ones who crucify. This is what is meant when the Christian faith affirms that man is made in the image of God, yet a sinner.

Secondly, we need the palm leaf of praise. We know a

great deal about praising ourselves and each other, but have we forgotten how to praise God? As we have been on our knees in penitence, we must leap to our feet in praise in response to what God has done on behalf of sinful man. He seals his love on the cross and in the resurrection of Jesus Christ. God has done something for us which we were powerless to do ourselves; he frees us from the old life to a new life in Christ. He raises us from death into life and guides us from darkness into light. The "Hosannas" of Palm Sunday become the "Alleluias" of Easter morn. Hosanna! Alleluia! Praise God in the highest!

PRAYER   *Come, O Triumphant Christ, as thou didst come in ancient Jerusalem. Enter into our cities, cast out the malpractices in our temples, challenge the leaders of our day, and show forth thy love in our lives. Grant that we may lay ourselves—all that we are and all that we hope to be—in obedient service before thee, to the honor and glory of thy holy name. Amen.*

69

BASIN AND EWER

SCRIPTURE   Jesus, knowing that the Father had given all things into his hands, and that he had come from God and was going to God, rose from supper, laid aside his garments, and girded himself with a towel. Then he poured water into a basin, and began to wash the disciples' feet, and to wipe them with the towel with which he was girded. (John 13:3-5.)

Though he was in the form of God, [he] did not count equality with God a thing to be grasped, but emptied himself, taking the form of a servant, being born in the likeness of men. And being found in human form he humbled himself and became obedient unto death, even death on a cross. (Phil. 2:6-8.)

MEDITATION   The symbols of basin and ewer call us to remember a significant event which happened during the last meal Jesus had with his disciples. During the meal Jesus quietly rose from eating, laid aside his garments, and girded himself with a towel. He used a ewer to pour water into a basin; then he began washing the disciples' feet. He who was their master assumed the role of a servant, and it scandalized the disciples. Peter refused to let Jesus wash his feet until Jesus warned him that he must have his feet washed to have a part in the ministry.

John's Gospel makes it perfectly clear that the act of foot-washing was a symbol which pointed beyond itself. In a

70

highly dramatic fashion, Jesus announced to his disciples that his role as the Messiah was as a servant. God, through Jesus Christ, came to sinful man in the form of a servant and desired to perform the ministry of reconciliation. Throughout his earthly ministry Jesus described his mission in terms of servant-hood. "The Son of man came not to be served but to serve, and to give his life as a ransom for many," he said at another time. Because Jesus was a servant—determined to serve even those who would not accept his ministry—he was marched to a cross, and even in his dying he performed a ministry of love. By emptying himself and taking on the form of a servant Jesus incarnated God's gracious action toward mankind from the very dawn of human history.

Jesus, in the act of footwashing, not only proclaimed the essence of his mission to the world, but also of his disciples' calling. They too must be servants.

"You call me Teacher and Lord; and you are right, for so I am. If I then, your Lord and Teacher, have washed your feet, you also ought to wash one another's feet. For I have given you an example, that you also should do as I have done to you. Truly, truly, I say to you, a servant is not greater than his master; nor is he who is sent greater than he who sent him." (John 13:13-16.)

As Christ was sent by the Father to minister unto his disciples, so they are sent to continue his witness to one another and to the world. By such a statement Jesus reminds us that the only valid response to God's gracious action is one of obedient service. We, as servants, are not above our Master. Jesus loved. So must we. Jesus preached. So must we. Jesus healed. So must we. Jesus suffered. So must we. Jesus taught. So

71

must we. Only by accepting his ministry to us and by ministering to our neighbors can we have any part of him who was called Christ. In obedient service we discover for ourselves what David Livingstone learned about Jesus:

He is the greatest Master I have ever known. If there is anyone greater, I do not know him. Jesus Christ is the only Master supremely worth serving. He is the only ideal that never loses its inspiration. He is the only friend whose friendship meets every demand. He is the only Savior who can save us to the uttermost. We go forth in His name, in His power, and in His Spirit, to serve Him.

PRAYER   *Almighty God, give us grace to be not only hearers but doers of thy holy word, not only to admire but to obey thy doctrine, not only to love but to live thy gospel. So grant that what we learn of thy glory we may receive into our hearts and show forth in our lives, through Jesus Christ our Lord. Amen.*

CUP AND CROSS

SCRIPTURE   And they went to a place which was called Gethsemane; and he said to his disciples, "Sit here, while I pray." And he took with him Peter and James and John, and began to be greatly distressed and troubled. And he said to them, "My soul is very sorrowful, even to death; remain here, and watch." And going a little farther, he fell on the ground and prayed that, if it were possible, the hour might pass from him. And he said, "Abba, Father, all things are possible to thee; remove this cup from me; yet not what I will, but what thou wilt." (Mark 14:32-37.)

MEDITATION   The American poet Sidney Lanier caught the mood of what happened in Gethsemane's garden:

> Into the woods my Master went,
> Clean forspent, forspent.
> Into the woods my Master came,
> Forspent with love and shame.
> But the olives they were not blind to Him,
> The little gray leaves were kind to Him:
> The thorn-tree had a mind to Him
> When into the woods he came.
>
> Out of the woods my Master went,
> And He was well content.
> Out of the woods my Master came,
> Content with death and shame.
> When Death and Shame would woo Him last,
> From under the trees they drew Him last:
> 'Twas on a tree they slew Him—last
> When out of the woods He came.

A transformation took place in Gethsemane. Jesus went into the woods forspent, but he came out of the woods well content. The Gospels indicate that this is true. As Jesus entered the garden, Mark describes him as "greatly distressed

73

and troubled." Jesus spoke of his soul's being very sorrowful, even to death. When he came out of the Garden, he was reconciled to the task of reconciliation. He faced his tormentors, accusers, enemies, with a forgiving love which triumphed even in the tragedy of the cross.

The cup and cross symbolize what happened in Gethsemane. It is significant that in Christian symbolism the cross is shown as connected with the cup. The cup which Jesus had to drink was death on a cross. It was no easy decision to make. Luke, in the parallel passage, pictures Jesus praying in such agony that "his sweat became like great drops of blood falling down upon the ground" (22:44). Jesus was at the crowning day of manhood; he was in good physical health; and he wanted to live. To desire death on the cross would have been morbid and unhealthy. Jesus the man did not want to die, but Jesus the Christ understood that it was his vocation to die. In Gethsemane we see the eternal struggle which takes place in every man between desire and duty. In Jesus the conflict was resolved perfectly in the prayer of dedication: "Yet not what I will, but what thou wilt." God's will became Jesus' will, and Jesus' will became God's will. Unwillingly at first, then willingly, Jesus took the cup of pain, sorrow, rejection, and death.

When pictured alone the cup symbolizes the Lord's Supper and reminds us that Jesus took bread and broke it, took wine and poured it into a cup, and gave these elements to his disciples. When Christians participate in the Lord's Supper today we are receiving from God's hands his grace that will strengthen us for the tasks which we have been called to perform in our world. The cup which is given to us at worship also has behind it a cross. When we receive, as unworthy servants, we ask that God's will might be done in our lives and that we might share Christ's cross. There is an agony in such a decision, but how the ecstacy overshadows it!

PRAYER   *Our Father, we confess that we have wanted thee, but not enough to make sacrifices. We have prayed that thy will might be done on earth, but we have been reluctant to accept thy will for our lives. We have seen the fault in our neighbors, but have been blind to our own shortcomings. Forgive the double character of our lives and make us one person in one Church under one Lord, even Jesus Christ. Amen.*

LANTERN AND TORCH
SWORD AND STAFF

SCRIPTURE   So Judas, procuring a band of soldiers and some officers from the chief priests and the Pharisees, went there with lanterns and torches and weapons. Then Jesus, knowing all that was to befall him, came forward and said to them, "Whom do you seek?" They answered him, "Jesus of Nazareth." Jesus said to him, "I am he." . . . So the band of soldiers and their captain and the officers of the Jews seized Jesus and bound him. (John 18:3-5, 12.)

MEDITATION   Think of the countless people who came to Jesus. In the opening chapter of John's Gospel Andrew and another disciple of the Baptist came to Jesus. Later Andrew brought Simon Peter to Jesus. They wanted to be his disciples and follow him the rest of their lives. Nicodemus, the Pharisee, came to Jesus with the burning question of how he could be saved. Mary and Martha sent for him to heal Lazarus, their brother. At another time some Greeks came to Philip with the request, "Sir, we wish to see Jesus." All had one thing in common: They came to Jesus with open spirits. But other people came to Jesus with dark purposes in mind. The Pharisees came to trap him; the Zealots came to force him to be an earthly king; pious Jews came to stone him; and finally, soldiers and officers from the chief priests came to arrest him. Lanterns, torches, swords, and staffs have become poignant reminders that some come to Jesus in order to do him violence. They do not want to hear his word, for they have already made up their minds about him. He is a troublemaker. . . . He is a madman. . . . He is a revolutionary. . . . He is a fraud. . . .

It is impossible to come into the presence of Jesus as a casual, neutral observer. He calls us to decision. When he said that he had come to bring war, not peace Jesus emphasized the division which the gospel creates. This is particularly evident in lands where Christianity is rivaled by pagan religions. In Japan son has been thrown against father and mother because he embraced Christianity while they remained Buddhists. The decision is an either/or choice. Either we find in Jesus, the Christ, who holds the ultimate meaning for us, or we do not.

The question for us is, how do we come to Jesus? Do we come with our minds already made up about him, based on what others have told us? This is the way which the soldiers and officers from the chief priests came. To them it was an open and shut case. Jesus was a dangerous man who had to be arrested and stopped at all costs. The Romans saw him as a threat to the imperial control of Rome, and the Jews felt he was destroying the traditional faith. Their hearts and minds were closed to any possibility that Jesus could be the one whom the prophets foretold. And nothing would convince them—even if he rose from the dead! There is another way to come, as evidenced by Andrew, Simon Peter, Nicodemus, Mary and Martha, and the Greeks. We may come to Jesus opened to the possibility that in him is the end of all our searching and the goal of all of our longing. We may come to Jesus and allow him to speak his redeeming word to us—not with lanterns and torches, swords and staffs, but with empty hands waiting to receive. The testimony of the disciples of all ages is that no one who comes to him is ever disappointed—no one!

PRAYER   *Our heavenly Father, we adore thee, whose name is love, whose nature is compassion, whose presence is joy, whose word is truth, whose spirit is goodness, whose holiness is beauty, whose will is peace, whose service is perfect freedom, and in the knowledge of whom standeth our eternal life. Praise be unto thee for thy great goodness and steadfast love which is with us all the days of our lives; through Jesus Christ our Lord. Amen.*

77

COCK

SCRIPTURE   Now Peter was sitting outside in the court-yard. And a maid came to him, and said, "You also were with Jesus the Galilean." But he denied it before them all, saying, "I do not know what you mean." And when he went out to the porch, another maid saw him, and she said to the by-standers, "This man was with Jesus of Nazareth." And again he denied it with an oath, "I do not know the man." After a little while the bystanders came up and said to Peter, "Certainly you are also one of them, for your accent betrays you." Then he began to invoke a curse on himself and to swear, "I do not know the man." And immediately the cock crowed. And Peter remembered the saying of Jesus, "Before the cock crows, you will deny me three times." And he went out and wept bitterly. (Matt. 26:69-75.)

MEDITATION   A cock's crowing smashed the proud, self-assured manner of the Apostle Peter like pottery. Before the arrest of Jesus Peter pointed at his fellow disciples and said to Jesus, "Though they all fall away because of you, I will never fall away" (Matt. 26:33). Jesus told him that he would. Unmoved by Jesus' realism, Peter reinforced his pledge of allegiance: "Even if I must die with you, I will not deny you" (vs. 35). And Matthew records, "And so said all the disciples." The cock's crowing was more than a symbol of

Peter's denial. It was a rousing reminder of all the disciples' denial. Every last man of them fled for safety into the dark night—away from the search party with lanterns and swords, away from the soldiers with nails and crosses, away from suffering and death. They had learned, as Dietrich Bonhoeffer once said, that grace is costly, not cheap. They wanted only cheap grace.

The cock represented in the stained glass of our sanctuaries stands as an unwelcome reminder that the denial of the first disciples is our denial as well. Although we live in a different historical situation, our denial is no less real or tragic. Professing to follow Christ with our lips, we have denied him with our lives. We have been perfectly willing to be Christians when it is fashionable, but we run away when our profession becomes unpopular.

What are the dynamics of our denial? It would be impossible to list here the specific ways we deny Jesus Christ, for they are too numerous and are bound up within our individual lives. Suffice it to say that we deny Christ whenever we build our lives around any meaning other than that revealed in him. God has a total claim on us, and we are called to respond in faithful obedience. When we attempt to escape this claim and to make claims of our own we deny the God who comes to us in Jesus Christ. This is what happened to the early disciples. Jesus said, "Come, follow me." It became increasingly clearer that he was not inviting them to a picnic, but to a cross. The disciples were told to leave all—father, mother, sisters, brothers, social status—to follow him. When the chips were down, however, they refused to find the meaning of their lives in Jesus' cross, choosing to search elsewhere. They placed transitory concerns before the claim of Jesus on their lives. The basis of denial is the same today. We still place ourselves at the center and attempt to find meaning from our own impoverished resources.

PRAYER   *We have denied thee, O Lord, but thou hast never denied us. In the face of our faithlessness thou hast been faithful, and our rejection of thee has been met by thine acceptance of us. Forgive us, we humbly beseech thee, for large professions and small deeds, for denial which we call expediency, and for unwillingness to be changed. Grant that we might remember who thou didst intend for us to be, and aid us in so becoming; through Jesus Christ. Amen.*

MONEY BAG AND COINS

SCRIPTURE   Then one of the twelve, who was called Judas Iscariot, went to the chief priests and said, "What will you give me if I deliver him to you?" And they paid him thirty pieces of silver. And from that moment he sought an opportunity to betray him. (Matt. 26:14-16.)

When Judas, his betrayer, saw that he was condemned, he repented and brought back the thirty pieces of silver to the chief priests and the elders, saying, "I have sinned in betraying innocent blood." They said, "What is that to us? See to it yourself." And throwing down the pieces of silver in the temple, he departed; and he went and hanged himself. (Matt. 27:3-5.)

MEDITATION   Money bags and coins are symbols which stand for the betrayal of Christ by Judas Iscariot. Behind these symbols lives the tragic tale of a man whose name is uttered in contempt.

Although Judas finally came to be considered as the chief villain among the disciples, he did not begin his association with Jesus as a recognizable traitor. Obviously from the Gospel accounts, he was a man of ability and was greatly trusted. We can be sure that he would not have been treasurer for the apostles if there had been an ounce of doubt about his character! If the disciples believed anyone capable of betraying Christ they suspected themselves individually. At the last meal when Jesus said, "Someone will betray me," everyone of them asked, "Lord, is it I?" They were realistic to know that the seeds of betrayal were planted in every heart and could easily spring to fruition.

What caused Judas to betray Jesus? The traditional answer has always been because of the money he received, hence the symbol of money bags and coins. Yet this is really an inadequate answer, for thirty pieces of silver was not enough money to make the treachery profitable. Some deeper motive must be sought. Perhaps the key to his treachery is found in his name—Iscariot. Some scholars have suggested that the name is connected with *sicarius,* a group of fanatical Jewish nationalists. If this is so, then Judas saw Jesus through eyes filled with hate and hope—hate of the Roman occupation

81

forces and hope for the establishment of Israel as a world power. He thought that Jesus as the Messiah would set up an earthly kingdom and destroy the enemy. How excitement must have mounted within Judas as Jesus came into the city of Jerusalem in triumph. Soon, Judas must have thought, he will establish his kingdom! But when Jesus only continued to speak of suffering and death, perhaps Judas sought to force his hand by bringing the authorities down on him. The real tragedy of Judas is that he worked his treachery honestly believing that his deed was in the best interests of both Israel and Jesus. It soon became apparent that he was a traitor, and he committed suicide.

The sin of Judas was misplaced faith. He had painted his own picture of a Messiah and had tried to make Jesus Christ fit his portrait. Judas consistently refused to hear the word which Jesus spoke about himself, preferring to stay within the warm cocoon of his dream. Such is our sin, for we try to make Jesus fit into our pattern. We make him into a national god in times of conflict; we call upon him to approve our customs and often think of him as an American export.

Jesus Christ comes as the dream shatterer, calling us to give up our preconceived ideas and to encounter him as he is. To insist on clutching our words when confronted by his word is to betray him again, but to receive him in faith is to crown him Lord of all.

PRAYER   *Open our minds, O God, to the true nature of thy revelation in Jesus Christ our Lord. Forgive us for our hesitancy to confront thee, our rebellion against thy will, and our smug satisfaction with life. Shatter our vain illusions and bring us face to face with reality, even the reality found in Jesus Christ. Amen.*

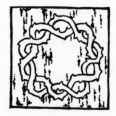

CROWN OF THORNS

SCRIPTURE   Then the soldiers of the governor took Jesus into the praetorium, and they gathered the whole battalion before him. And they stripped him and put a scarlet robe upon him, and plaiting a crown of thorns they put it on his head, and put a reed in his right hand. And kneeling before him they mocked him, saying, "Hail, King of the Jews!" And they spat upon him, and took the reed and struck him on the head. And when they had mocked him, they stripped him of the robe, and put his own clothes on him, and led him away to crucify him. (Matt. 27:27-31.)

MEDITATION   A crown of thorns was the only earthly crown Jesus Christ ever wore; yet we hail him as "King of kings and Lord of lords." He appears in his suffering and death as one who is weak; yet in him we find the strength of the ages. In the closing chapters of the Gospels which describe his passion, we find Christ standing powerless in front of his tormentors and judges. The soldiers mock him with military cruelty. The crowd yells their hate at him. The Pharisees gloat over his dying. It is paradoxical that we believe in the power of God; yet we look upon the crucified Messiah as the chief revelation of God's power. G. A. Studdert-Kennedy put it in moving verse:

83

> God, the God I love and worship, reigns in sorrow
>   on the Tree,
> Broken, bleeding, but unconquered, very God of
>   God to me.
> All that showy pomp of splendour, all that sheen
>   of angel wings,
> Was not borrowed from the baubles that surround
>   our earthly kings.

.   .   .   .

> . . . for Thy glory is the glory of Love's loss,
> And Thou hast no other splendour but the splen-
>   dour of the Cross.

.   .   .   .

> On my knees I fall and worship that great Cross
>   that shines above,
> For the very God of Heaven is not Power, but
>   Power of Love.

Perhaps the paradox is resolved when we realize that God's power is not raw, naked power which engulfs man whether or not he wills it, but rather the power of love which woos man and leaves him the freedom of decision. God is powerful in his weakness, and the crown of thorns shines like glittering gold.

Why does God choose to be weak in his world rather than strong? Why did he come to a humble stable instead of riding on clouds of glory? Why did he die on a cross when he could have lived in pomp more dazzling than any earthly king? Because God loves man and seeks to bring us, like the prodigal sons we are, back to our rightful home. His weakness is the self-imposed weakness of love. Raw power does not conquer men's hearts and minds, even though it may exact token allegiance. Victorious armies are able to control occupied territory, however they are unable to force love from the citizens. God as power and justice and wrath may awe men, but he does not win their love. Only God as weakness and forgiveness and love can accomplish the work of redemption. Only the God who comes to us in Jesus Christ can cause rebellious man to lay down his arms and take up a doxology. Charles Wesley knew this full well. In his magnificent hymn on the passion of Christ he sang out:

> The Son of God for me hath died:
> My Lord, my Love, is crucified:
> Is crucified for me and you,
> To bring us rebels back to God.

PRAYER   *O merciful God, who art the Lord of creation, and who hatest nothing that thou hast created, we know that thou willest not the death of a sinner, but rather that he should be led to new life in thee. Have mercy upon all who deny the faith of Christ crucified. Take from them all hardness of heart and ignorance of thy Word; return them to a right relationship with thee in the fellowship of thy holy church. And to thee be all power, honor, dominion, and glory both now and forever. Amen.*

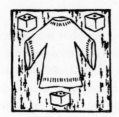

SEAMLESS ROBE
AND DICE

SCRIPTURE   When the soldiers had crucified Jesus they took his garments and made four parts, one for each soldier. But his tunic was without seam, woven from top to bottom; so they said to one another, "Let us not tear it, but cast lots for it to see whose it shall be." This was to fulfill the scripture.

"They parted my garments among them,
and for my clothing they cast lots."

So the soldiers did this. (John 19:23-25a.)

MEDITATION   The soldiers were more interested in what Jesus left behind than they were in Jesus. For them Jesus was another man they had been ordered to put to death. They were carrying out their orders and that was that. Unlike the Pharisees, who taunted the man who hung helpless on the cross, the soldiers turned their attention to his garments. They couldn't have cared less about Jesus. In Christian art, the seamless robe and dice symbolize the soldiers gambling at the foot of the cross. It is a tragic scene indeed. Yet these soldiers were not the only—nor even the principal—gamblers on Golgotha's hill. G. A. Studdert-Kennedy has reminded us of the whole truth:

> And, sitting down, they watched Him there,
> The soldiers did;
> There, while they played with dice,

He made His Sacrifice,
And died upon the Cross to rid
God's world of sin.
He was a gambler too, my Christ,
He took His life and threw
It for a world redeemed.
And e'er His agony was done,
Before the westering sun went down,
Crowning that day with its crimson crown,
He knew that He had won.

In contrast to the soldiers, Christ made the greatest wager of all. He bet his life that truth conquers falsehood, that good overcomes evil, and that the lance of love pierces the wall of hate. At the foot of the cross, the soldiers engaged in cheap, immoral gambling. On the cross, Jesus took a heroic chance with his life.

The spirit of adventure and enterprise is a virtue, not a vice. Gambling, when it is not perverted into a game of chance, is a natural part of human nature. Indeed, Christ calls us to be adventurous gamblers for God. Too long our Christian response has been cautious, careful, and conservative. We have warmed our hands by the fires of tradition, refusing to face the cold winds outside the camp. Instead of being identified with progress and courage, the church has become equated with the status quo and timidity. Now is the time—pray that it is not too late—for the body of Christ to play long shots against overwhelming odds of evil. We must dare speak out for unpopular causes if these causes will forward the coming of Christ's reign in all the complex relationships of life. One of the greatest gamblers in the long history of Christianity was Martin Luther. When the church was at a low ebb, corrupted and complacent, he gambled everything to return it to its true nature. Hauled before the great men of the land and called on to stop his criticism, the great monk boomed his defiance: "Here I stand. I cannot do otherwise. God help me. Amen." From Martin Luther's gamble of faith came the great Reformation and the Protestant way of life. Perhaps another great Reformation will come today if enough of us are willing to take some chances.

PRAYER   *O God, who has placed in our hearts such deep desires that we cannot be at rest until we rest in thee, we do not pray for personal peace, but for righteousness. Set our sights on the unseen and the eternal, open our minds to the counsels of thy eternal wisdom, grant us adventuresome spirits. O Lord, give us grace to seek first the establishment of thy kingdom, and we know that thou wilt supply all things needful for our lives. In the name of him who came as a light unto the world, even Jesus Christ our Lord, we pray. Amen.*

CROSS

SCRIPTURE   So they took Jesus, and he went out, bearing his own cross, to the place called the place of a skull, which is called in Hebrew Golgotha. There they crucified him, and with him two others, one on either side, and Jesus between them. Pilate also wrote a title and put it on the cross; it read, "Jesus of Nazareth, the King of the Jews." (John 19:17-19.)

For God so loved the world that he gave his only Son, that whoever believes in him should not perish but have eternal life. For God sent the Son into the world, not to condemn the world, but that the world might be saved through him. (John 3:16-17.)

MEDITATION   On the dark, windswept hill of Golgotha came the climax of the events of betrayal, arrest, and trial. Deserted by his disciples and surrounded by a jeering mob, the God-Man, Jesus, hung helpless on a crude, wooden cross. The Pharisees shouted the paradox, "He saved others; he cannot save himself!"

Remembering the scene, a little girl asked, "Where was God when they crucified Jesus?" How could a loving God allow Jesus to die? is another way of asking the question. There is no easy answer, as evidenced by many complex theories of the atonement. Perhaps the truest answer to the question is simply that God was there. Jesus died because

89

God was a loving God, and in his dying, he changed the cross from a symbol of hate to one of his love. Today the cross is a central symbol in most Protestant sanctuaries; it towers above our steeples, and it casts a shadow on church lawns. Christians have come to see in the cross a loving God who participates in our lives—in our suffering and in our dying —and who allows himself to be made weak in order that we might be made strong.

Marc Connelly captured the truth of the cross in his play *The Green Pastures*. God turned away a delegation that had come to persuade him to help his people on the earth, but he finally decides to go to his people. In the final scene of the play he is talking with Gabriel. God has been thinking:

'Bout somethin' de boy tol' me. Somethin' 'bout Hosea, and himself. How dey foun' somethin'.
GABRIEL. What, Lawd?
GOD. Mercy. (*A pause*) Through *sufferin'*, he said. . . . I'm tryin' to find it, too. It's awful impo'tant. It's awful impo'tant to all de people on my earth. Did he mean dat even God must suffer?

A voice in the distance is heard: "Oh, look at him! Oh, look, dey goin' to make him carry it up dat high hill! Dey goin' to nail him to it! Oh, dat's a terrible burden for one man to carry!"

It is a terrible burden for one man to carry. The cross comes to us in our day, not only as a symbol of God's love toward us, but also as a call to decision. We are called to share —in the present moment—Christ's cross. To share his cross means that we will suffer for our neighbor's sake, that we will accept life as God gives it to us, that we will live as men of faith. If we respond and share his cross we will discover that we do not carry his burden alone, for he is still alongside us. He bears the burden with us and for us. "Take my yoke upon you, and learn from me; for I am gentle and lowly in heart, and you will find rest for your souls. For my yoke is easy, and my burden is light." (Matt. 11:29-30.)

PRAYER   *Our Father who art in heaven, thy name is perfect love; for us men and for our salvation thou camest down from heaven and wast made man. Thou sharest fully in our existence, tasting rejection, disappointment, and even death. May we share in thy sacrifice as true disciples so that all honor, power, and glory be thine forever and ever. Amen.*

RESURRECTION SYMBOLS

SCRIPTURE   But in fact Christ has been raised from the dead, the first fruits of those who have fallen asleep. For as by a man came death, by a man has come also the resurrection of the dead. For as in Adam all die, so also in Christ shall all be made alive. . . . The sting of death is sin, and the power of sin is the law. But thanks be to God, who gives us the victory through our Lord Jesus Christ. (I Cor. 15:20-22, 56-57.)

MEDITATION   A cluster of symbols hangs around the Resurrection of Jesus Christ. On the face of them, some seem to be odd and inappropriate. As we examine them more closely, however, we see that every last symbol represents the essential truth of the Resurrection—newness of life.

The lily is a symbol familiar to most of us because it graces our churches on Easter Sunday. The wax throats of the lily proclaim that Jesus is risen. As a symbol of Easter, the lily refers to the fact that a dead bulb in the soil produces a new bulb, stem, leaves, and flowers, all rising above the soil. Even though the bulb decays—the bulb symbolizing our earthly bodies—a new life comes from it.

A bursting pomegranate stands for the hope of new life because it is split open by the pressure of many seeds. This symbolizes the power to reproduce life.

Another resurrection symbol is a mythical bird known as the phoenix. This bird was supposed to have risen from the ashes of the fire in which it had been destroyed and therefore was regarded as a fitting reminder of resurrection.

A common symbol of the resurrection in the early church was a peacock. After a peacock molts he grows new feathers more beautiful than those he lost.

The butterfly is another symbol for the resurrection. In the chrysalis stage it is apparently without life, but then it bursts the cocoon prison and soars into the sky with a pair of beautiful wings. So it is that the human body, after death, is committed to the ground, but the personality is resurrected to everlasting life.

On Friday, the powers of evil did their worst, and Jesus Christ died on a cross reserved for criminals. On Sunday morning, however, God did his best and brought death under dominion in the person of the crucified and risen Lord of life. "He's alive," shouted the Captain in Charles Rann Kennedy's play *The Terrible Meek*. "He's alive. I can't kill him. All the empires can't kill him." Jesus Christ, crucified, dead, and buried, received new life and offers life to everyone who believes. His resurrection inaugurated a new age for man. As Paul put it: "For as in Adam all die, so also in Christ shall all be made alive" (I Cor. 15:22). Left to himself, a creature estranged from God, man is doomed to die, but as a creature reconciled to God, man is free to live. The marvelous message of Easter is that you can have new life in the present moment. You need not wait for some tomorrow to taste the victory which Christ proclaims. It is a present reality for you. The question of Easter is not in the future tense: Will I live with Christ after I die? The question is: Am I alive to Christ now? Have I heard his word to me and responded in obedience?

PRAYER   *O God, who through the resurrection of Jesus Christ hast freed us from the power of darkness and brought us into the kingdom of thy love; grant, we beseech thee, that, as by his death he has recalled us into life, so by his abiding presence he may bring us to the joys eternal; through him who for our sakes died and rose again, and is ever with us in power, the same Jesus Christ our Lord. Amen.*

V

MEDITATIONS ON SYMBOLS
OF NEW TESTAMENT
PERSONALITIES

PETER

SCRIPTURE   When they had finished breakfast, Jesus said to Simon Peter, "Simon, son of John, do you love me more than these?" He said to him, "Yes, Lord; you know that I love you." He said to him, "Feed my lambs." A second time he said to him, "Simon, son of John, do you love me?" He said to him, "Yes, Lord; you know that I love you." He said to him, "Tend my sheep." He said to him a third time, "Simon, son of John, do you love me?" Peter was grieved because he said to him the third time, "Do you love me?" And he said to him, "Lord, you know everything; you know that I love you." Jesus said to him, "Feed my sheep." (John 21:15-17.)

MEDITATION   Peter was a vast continent of a man. Big, bustling, boisterous, he walks through the pages of the New Testament with a giant stride. We know more about his life than any of the other apostles; he is always named first in the apostolic lists; and he is obviously in second command to Jesus. When Jesus first met Peter the apostle's name was Simon. Jesus saw in Simon tremendous potential as a bulwark for the good news. So he changed his name to Peter, which means rock.

Simon Peter sometimes appears to us a rolling rock, an unsteady, imperfect man who misrepresented the message and mission of Jesus. At one point Jesus even sees Satan working in Peter's ignorance. The symbol of a cock reminds us of Peter, for he denied his Lord three times before morning brought the cock's crowing. We last encounter Peter in John's Gospel on a dramatic occasion. The risen Christ is restoring him to apostleship. For every time Peter denied the Christ on that night of horror Christ demanded that he reaffirm his love. More than this, Jesus told him how he could prove his love—by feeding the flock which Jesus had called out from the world, by being a faithful servant to all. In his dialogue between Jesus and Peter we find the essence of our condition. Like Peter, we have denied our Lord. Still the Denied One comes to us, his body pierced by the fresh marks of crucifixion, and he speaks his word of forgiveness. No harsh condemnation falls from his lips, only forgiveness. It is difficult for us sinful men to receive this forgiveness, for we recognize our unworthiness. To refuse forgiveness when it is offered is only to deny him again and to multiply the contradictions of our situation; while to accept his forgiveness is to find restoration in the company of the committed and to begin each day anew as forgiven, free men.

When we see Peter at Pentecost he is no longer a rolling rock. The gathered crowd is amazed by his preaching, and many come to receive the forgiveness which Peter proclaims to be theirs in Jesus Christ. Later Peter is faithful even unto death. Early church tradition believes that Peter went to Rome about A.D. 61. In danger of his life, Peter was fleeing from the city when he saw his Lord coming into Rome. "Lord," he said, "whither goest thou?"

The Lord answered, "I go into Rome to be crucified."

"Lord," said Peter, "art thou being crucified again?"

"Yea, Peter," said the Lord, "I am being crucified again."

Peter realized that the Lord was going into Rome to carry the cross from which he was fleeing. So he turned back to die. On his shield is an inverted cross, for by his request he was crucified head downward, and not as Jesus. The crossed keys refer to Peter's confession of faith in Christ and his receiving the "keys of the kingdom" (Matt. 16:18-19).

PRAYER   *Father in heaven! Hold not our sins up against us but hold us up against our sins, so that the thought of thee when it wakens in our soul, and each time it wakens should not remind us of what we have committed but of what Thou didst forgive, not of how we went astray but of how Thou didst save us! Amen.*

 ANDREW

SCRIPTURE   The next day again John was standing with two of his disciples; and he looked at Jesus as he walked, and said, "Behold, the Lamb of God!" The two disciples heard him say this, and they followed Jesus. . . . One of the two who heard John speak, and followed him, was Andrew, Simon Peter's brother. He first found his brother Simon, and said to him, "We have found the Messiah" (which means Christ). He brought him to Jesus. (John 1:35-37, 40-42.)

MEDITATION   Andrew's claim to fame was that he made no claim to fame. He possessed the unusual ability to accept a secondary and obscure position with graciousness. John's Gospel shows that Andrew was one of the first disciples to meet Jesus. It was Andrew who brought his brother Peter to Jesus. Peter became the second-in-command of the band of disciples. Always Andrew is identified as "Simon Peter's brother." Such was probably the case even before Andrew and Peter became disciples. "There's Andrew, Simon's kid brother," neighbors probably said. Even though Andrew lived in the Rock's shadow, there is no trace of bitterness or jealousy in their relationship. Andrew was never a member of the inner circle of the apostles; still he did what he could when he could. He did not care who received the credit; getting the job done was the important concern.

The first three Gospels do not mention Andrew except in the lists of the apostles. John's Gospel is the one which paints a clear picture of him. He comes to the foreground on three occasions, and every time he is bringing someone to Jesus. First he brought Peter to Jesus. At another time Andrew brought a little lad with five loaves and two fishes to Jesus (John 6:8-9). Finally we see Andrew bringing the Greeks to Jesus. He saw as his mission in life bringing others to Jesus, throwing the spotlight on his master instead of on himself. Is there any greater wisdom on the meaning of Christian discipleship?

Three countries—Russia, Greece, and Scotland—claim Andrew as their patron saint. Tradition portrays him as a great missionary, carrying on work in Cappadocia, Bithynia,

Galatia, and Byzantium. His name is especially connected with the barbarous Scythians, whose land corresponds to part of modern Russia.

Andrew's emblem is an X-like cross, the four ends touching the edges of the shield. According to the early church historian Eusebius, Andrew died at Petrae, a city of Achaia, at the hands of Aegeas, the proconsul, on November 30, A.D. 60. Andrew had gained many converts by his preaching, including the proconsul's wife and brother. Aegeas, furious at wholesale abandonment of the gods, ordered Andrew to bow down to the gods and recall the people to their old way of worship. Andrew flatly refused. So he was scourged with rods, mounted on a cross, and left to die. In order to make his death more horrible, he was not nailed to the cross, but bound, and left to die of hunger, thirst, and exposure. According to legend, Andrew asked to be bound to an X-shaped cross because he was unworthy to die on the same type of cross as his master. In Andrew's death as in his life, he found Jesus and by his witness brought others to him. Nothing more—and nothing less—is demanded of us.

PRAYER *Hail, precious cross! Thou hast been consecrated by the body of my Lord and adorned with his limbs as rich jewels. I come to thee exulting and glad. Receive me with joy into thine arms. O good cross, thou hast received beauty from our Lord's limbs. I have ardently loved thee. Long have I desired and sought thee. Now thou art found by me, and art made ready for my longing soul. Receive me into thine arms; take me up from among men, and present me to my Master, that he who redeemed me on thee may receive me by thee. Amen.*

> —Traditional prayer of Andrew as he faced the cross on which he died

JAMES THE GREATER

SCRIPTURE   And James and John, the sons of Zebedee, came forward to him, and said to him, "Teacher, we want you to do for us whatever we ask of you." And he said to them, "What do you want me to do for you?" And they said to him, "Grant us to sit, one at your right hand and one at your left, in your glory." But Jesus said to them, "You do not know what you are asking. Are you able to drink the cup that I drink, or be baptized with the baptism with which I am baptized?" And they answered, "We are able." (Mark 10:35-45.)

About that time Herod the king laid violent hands upon some who belonged to the church. He killed James the brother of John with the sword. (Acts 12:1.)

MEDITATION   James the Greater was the brother of John, the son of Zebedee. Strangely we know very little about his life, although he seems to have been a disciple of no mean importance. Reading the Gospel lists of disciples, we find that James's name always appears in the first three in every list. The problem with James is that he never once appears apart from his brother John. Always, the Gospels speak of James and John doing this, James and John doing that. These men appear as a composite figure, Siamese twins who were not separated. Only in Acts does James the Greater emerge as an individual, and this is when he is put to death at the hands

102

of Herod Agrippa. In contrast to James, John went to Ephesus where he lived out his years in peace, dying as an old man.

The shield of James usually has on it three scallop shells, symbolic of his pilgrimages and missionary journeys. Two other symbols are also used. One is a pilgrim's staff with a hook and wallet hung on it; the other is a sword and a scallop shell, the sword reminding us that he was beheaded at the command of Herod.

James, along with his brother John, presented one of the most brash requests ever made to Jesus. Overlooking the gifts and graces of the other members of the apostolic band, they asked Jesus for chief places in the kingdom when he came into his glory. Unlike Andrew, they were pushers and grabbers. Jesus told them that they didn't know what they were asking. To inherit first places in the kingdom they must be satisfied with the last place. To save their lives they must lose them. "Only those go to heaven who are willing not to go." Jesus rules from a cross, not a throne, and to ask for places at his right and left hand is to ask for a sacrificial death. Although James and John answered they were able to drink of the cup of Jesus and to be baptized with his baptism, they did not understand what they were promising. Only later, when Jesus was arrested, tried, and crucified, did they discover that they were not able to follow him.

It is significant that James was the first of the apostles to become a martyr. In the company of Jesus his ambition for himself had changed to ambition for his Master. Having once failed to follow Jesus to his crucifixion under Pontius Pilate, James finally succeeded in following him. In losing his life he found it. He achieved one of the deepest desires of the human heart—to be identified with that which transcends human limitations. Eusebius records that the man who turned James over to Herod was so profoundly moved by the apostle's courageous behavior at his trial that the informer declared himself to be a Christian and received baptism from the apostle's hands. He, too, was tried and sentenced to die with James. As they were being led away to death he begged James's forgiveness. After a moment's pause the apostle gave him the kiss of peace and said, "Peace be unto thee." How like the one who said, "Father, forgive them."

PRAYER *O Lord Jesus Christ, we dare to pray: Make us able to drink the cup which thou didst drink and to be baptized with thy baptism. Help us to pour out our lives with the freedom of wine and water's flow for the service of our neighbors in thy name. Amen.*

JOHN

SCRIPTURE John answered, "Master, we saw a man casting out demons in your name, and we forbade him, because he does not follow with us." But Jesus said to him, "Do not forbid him; for he that is not against you is for you." (Luke 9:49-50.)

And he [Jesus] sent messengers ahead of him, who went and entered a village of the Samaritans . . . but the people would not receive him. . . . And when his disciples James and John saw it, they said, "Lord, do you want us to bid fire come down from heaven and consume them?" But he turned and rebuked them. And they went on to another village. (Luke 9:51b-56.)

MEDITATION   John holds an honored place in Christian history. Hundreds of churches have been named for him. A splendid host of Christian leaders have borne his name—such men as John Chrysostom, John Wycliffe, John Calvin, John Knox, John Wesley, and John Bunyan. The man for whom they were named was the son of Zebedee and the brother of James, a fisherman by trade, an apostle by calling. John joined Peter and James as the three members of the inner circle of the apostles. On the shield of John is a chalice and a serpent, which refers to the story of an attempt to kill him by poisoning. Tradition says that a priest of Diana gave John poisoned wine to drink, but he made the sign of the cross over the chalice, and the poison evaporated in the form of a serpent.

John was not a very likely candidate for the apostolic band. If we were members of a Committee on Apostolic Qualifications, I doubt that we would have given John a vote of confidence. He had made too many mistakes. He appeared as a man of great intolerance. He found a man casting out demons in the name of Jesus, but since the healer was not a member of their company, John told him to stop. Both he and his brother had violent, unruly tempers subject to explode at the slightest provocation. When met by Samaritan opposition to Jesus' passing through their village the brothers' solution to the problem was to call down fire. Kill off the opposition!

105

How unlike Jesus, who finally allowed the opposition to kill him off. James and John received a nickname because of their outbursts—Boanerges, meaning the sons of thunder. John becomes an even greater enigma when we consider that some scholars believe he was perhaps the closest disciple to Jesus. Many believe that the John of the Synoptics and the Beloved Disciple of the Fourth Gospel are the same man. These two are entirely different in character, however. The John of the Synoptics is an angry, intolerant man, while the Beloved Disciple is a figure of kindness and love. Does this not suggest that the two are two different men after all? Yes and no. Yes, in the sense that we have a picture of a changed man. No, in that both men are the Apostle John.

Jesus took John as he found him—brash, intolerant, angry —and guided him in using his characteristics for the service of the kingdom. Intolerance and anger are neutral qualities, neither bad nor good in themselves, but receiving their ethical color from how they are used in the concrete situations of life. On at least two occasions John used his intolerance and anger in a negative, destructive way that Jesus rejected. In the company of Jesus, however, John learned that intolerance and anger must come under the control of the law of love. Christians should be angry and intolerant when faced by disease, hunger, oppression, social injustice, hate, fear, ignorance—all things that thwart the dominion of Jesus Christ. The church needs more men like John!

PRAYER   *O God, grant that we not be intolerant and angry at men, but rather at the sin which imprisons them. Where there is darkness, may we cast light; where there is thirst, may we bring water; where there is hunger, may we spread food; where*

there is anxiety, may we bring peace; where there is sickness,
may we bring healing, remembering that if we say we love thee,
but do not love our neighbors, we are the worst of liars. Amen.

PHILIP

SCRIPTURE   The next day Jesus decided to go to Galilee.
And he found Philip and said to him, "Follow me." Now
Philip was from Bethsaida, the city of Andrew and Peter.
Philip found Nathanael, and said to him, "We have found
him of whom Moses in the law and also the prophets wrote,
Jesus of Nazareth, the son of Joseph." (John 1:43-45.)

Now among those who went up to worship at the feast
were some Greeks. So these came to Philip . . . and said to
him, "Sir, we wish to see Jesus." Philip went and told
Andrew; Andrew went with Philip and they told Jesus. (John
12:20-22.)

MEDITATION   In the Fourth Gospel Philip comes to life
as a real flesh and blood man with distinguishable characteristics. Heretofore he had been only a name tucked away
in the apostolic lists of the Synoptic Gospels. But John's

Gospel shines some light on him and gives us broad clues to his character.

First of all, we are told that Philip was from Bethsaida, the city of Andrew and Peter. This suggests that he was a fisherman by trade and possibly a close colleague of Andrew and Peter. He made his living by casting out nets and was certainly not a professional man.

Secondly, the Fourth Gospel records that Philip was the first man to whom Jesus addressed the words, "Follow me!" In the verses before Jesus meets Philip, we find Andrew hearing the master speak and running to tell his brother Simon about him. Then they both went to Jesus. But Jesus *came* to Philip and called him to discipleship. Thus Philip has the distinction not only of being the first disciple called, but also the first one to whom Jesus came personally.

We discover that Philip was a born missionary. When Philip had been found by Jesus he wasted no time in finding his friend Nathanael Bartholomew and telling him that the Messiah had come. He also demonstrated his talents by refusing to argue with Nathanael, but asking him simply, "Come and see." Meeting this kind of argument ends skepticism. At another time some Greeks came to him asking to see Jesus. Philip—unsure about what to do—went to Andrew, and both of them went to Jesus. It is probable that Philip and Andrew both led the Greeks to a meeting with Jesus.

Finally we discover that Philip was a man who was not afraid to ask Jesus questions. In the Upper Room Jesus was talking about the Father. Philip found the discourse difficult to follow, and blurted out, "Lord, show us the Father, and we shall be satisfied." Jesus' answer was clear and to the point: "He who has seen me has seen the Father." (See

John 14:6-11.) Philip, and the church after him, did not clearly understand this answer, but the Council of Nicea in A.D. 325 spelled it out definitely. The faith of the church was that Jesus Christ was "Very God of very God; Begotten, not made."

Legend records that Philip was crucified head downwards. The dying Philip asked that his body be wrapped in papyrus, not in linen, for he was not worthy that his dead body should receive the same treatment as the body of Jesus. On his shield is a thin cross and two loaves of bread, which remind us of John 6:7.

PRAYER *O Almighty God, who hast built thy Church upon the foundation of the Apostles and Prophets, Jesus Christ himself being the head corner-stone; Grant us so to be joined together in unity of spirit by their doctrine, that we may be made an holy temple acceptable unto thee; through the same Jesus Christ our Lord. Amen.*

BARTHOLOMEW

SCRIPTURE   Philip found Nathanael, and said to him, "We have found him of whom Moses in the law and also the prophets wrote, Jesus of Nazareth, the son of Joseph. Nathanael said to him, "Can anything good come out of Nazareth?" Philip said to him, "Come and see." Jesus saw Nathanael coming to him, and said of him, "Behold, an Israelite indeed, in whom there is no guile!" Nathanael said to him, "How do you know me?" Jesus answered him, "Before Philip called you, when you were under the fig tree, I saw you." Nathanael answered him, "Rabbi, you are the Son of God! You are the King of Israel!" (John 1:45-59.)

MEDITATION   Bartholomew and Nathanael are considered to be the same man. The first three Gospels always place Bartholomew alongside Philip in the list of apostles, which suggests they were close friends or perhaps even relatives. The Fourth Gospel never mentions Bartholomew at all, only Nathanael. When we encounter Nathanael, Philip is leading him to Jesus. In itself, Bartholomew is not a first name, but a surname. Bartholomew must have had a first name, and it was very possibly Nathanael. So this apostle can be called Nathanael Bartholomew.

If we were writing a play on our scripture it might well be entitled *From Bigotry to Belief*. When Philip told Nathanael that the Messiah had come from Nazareth his im-

110

mediate response was a sneer: "Can anything good come out of Nazareth?" Small wonder he asked this question, for Nazareth was what we would call "a wide place in the road." It was not mentioned in the Old Testament or the Talmud, and Nathanael expected a great man to come from a great city. He was prejudiced, closed to the possibility of greatness coming from smallness. Philip, with great wisdom, refused to argue the point with Nathanael. He knew that this would get him absolutely nowhere. Instead, he simply invited him to come and see. So Nathanael Bartholomew—bigoted, skeptical, suspicious—went along to take a look and received the surprise of his life. His wall of prejudice tumbled down. He exclaimed, "Rabbi, you are the Son of God! You are the King of Israel."

There are countless people today like Nathanael Bartholomew before he met Jesus. They prejudge Christ and even refuse to "come and see." The prejudiced ones think they know all there is to know about Christian faith, although their ideas are usually pitifully distorted. They have actually made more effort to understand what makes the garbage disposal work than who makes life work. Although they pretend to be open to truth, they are really quite closed. The gospels' word to the bigoted is, "Come and see. Be open to the new life offered in Jesus Christ." The only way to prove Christ is by following him; the only way to intellectually understand the Christian gospel is by making the "leap of faith." Encounter with him is what makes authentic life before God a present possibility. Bartholomew and the other apostles found this to be true. They all came, saw, and were conquered. They came as blind men, but in his service became men who could see.

111

The shield of Bartholomew symbolizes a believer, not a bigot. On it is a single flaying knife. Bartholomew was beheaded in Armenia for his Christian faith. He had learned that not only good, but God, came to him out of Nazareth.

PRAYER   *O Almighty and everlasting God, who didst give to thine Apostle Bartholomew grace truly to believe and to preach thy Word; Grant, we beseech thee, unto thy Church, to love that Word which he believed, and both to preach and receive the same; through Jesus Christ our Lord. Amen.*

THOMAS

SCRIPTURE   Now Thomas, one of the twelve, called the Twin, was not with them when Jesus came. So the other disciples told him, "We have seen the Lord." But he said to them, "Unless I see in his hands the print of the nails, and place my finger in the mark of the nails, and place my hand in his side, I will not believe." . . . Then he [Jesus] said to Thomas, "Put your finger here, and see my hands; and put out your hand, and place it in my side; do not be faithless, but believing." Thomas answered him, "My Lord and my God!" (John 20:24-25, 27-28.)

MEDITATION   We have really not treated Thomas fairly. Down through the ages, Christians have remembered him in a negative way as doubting Thomas. Often when a child displays an inquisitive mind about the faith, we hush-hush his questions by calling him "a doubting Thomas" and referring to the story in John's Gospel. So it is that many adults believe that doubt is sinful and the opposite of faith. Such, however, is not the case, for honest doubt is the other side of faith's coin. As Alfred, Lord Tennyson wrote:

> There lives more faith in honest doubt,
> Believe me, than in half the creeds.

We do not have too much doubt, but too little of it. Our faith is uncritical, capable of being blown to and fro by every wind of doctrine. Our problem is not that we don't believe in anything, but that we believe in everything. One business-man said rather cynically, "You can sell people on anything!" There is an element of truth in this statement, for we are people who want to be sold. Into the house of our faith creeps lie after lie simply because we fail to keep doubt as the door-keeper. It is impossible to have a vital and relevant Christian faith without the services of doubt.

Significantly, in our text, Jesus did not criticize Thomas for having doubts. He recognized this as a legitimate part of seeking, asking, and finding. Jesus was a doubter too. This is precisely what caused his clashes with the Pharisees. He doubted that their rules and regulations constituted God's demand upon man. It was Thomas' doubt that led him into deeper faith in Jesus Christ, not his acceptance of secondhand evidence. And this is the case in our lives. Doubt does not necessarily destroy faith and lead to despair; it can actually nourish it and guide us into a more adequate faith. In this sense doubt can be seen as a servant of faith.

There is, of course, a difference between honest and dishonest doubt, and it is our responsibility to be honest in our doubting—as honest as Thomas. Dishonest doubt closes all doors to inquiry, affirming the answer before ever attempting the discipline of finding an answer. Dishonest doubt is an uninterested doubt, which views the question of life from a safe distance. On the other hand, honest doubt involves the total person in the urgency of life. He realizes that he must fight for life, sink or swim, do or die. Again, honest doubt will force us to answer the question, "How shall we live as human beings?" The relationship between belief and action will become crystal clear. The question becomes, Is your doubt honest? If so, praise be to God!

Thomas was a rebel and a doubter, and Jesus Christ needs such men. This apostle became a missionary to India and established Christianity in that country. His shield pictures a carpenter's square and a vertical spear since, according to tradition, he built a church with his own hands and was put to death with a spear.

PRAYER   *Gracious God, thou who art the author of all truth, we thank thee for the discipline of doubt which leads to an acknowledgment of thy sovereignty. Bless all honest inquiry in our schools and universities. Give thy grace to all those who are in these communities of learning, both professors and students. And with Thomas, may we all truly say of Jesus Christ, "My Lord and my God!" Amen.*

114

MATTHEW

SCRIPTURE   As Jesus passed on from there, he saw a man called Matthew sitting at the tax office; and he said to him, "Follow me." And he rose and followed him.

And as he sat at table in the house, behold, many tax collectors and sinners came and sat down with Jesus and his disciples. And when the Pharisees saw this, they said to his disciples, "Why does your teacher eat with tax collectors and sinners?" But when he heard it, he said, "Those who are well have no need of a physician, but those who are sick. Go and learn what this means, 'I desire mercy, and not sacrifice.' For I came not to call the righteous, but sinners." (Matt. 9:9-13.)

MEDITATION   Matthew was universally hated because of his profession. He was a publican, or tax collector. In twentieth century language, this meant he was a "quisling," a "traitor," a "collaborationist." Matthew was a Jew who worked for the Roman government, milking taxes from his own people. For the pious Jew to pay tribute in this way was intolerable, since to pay such a tribute to anyone but God himself was considered an infringement upon God's domain. Tax collectors were also a dishonest lot, notorious for collecting more taxes than actually due and pocketing the difference. Murderers, robbers, and tax collectors were classed together. Tax collectors were not permitted to worship with the Jews, and repentance was even regarded as especially difficult for them. Pious Jews would spit on the ground as they passed the publican's place of business. Publicans were not allowed to live in the Jewish community, but had to dwell outside with the lepers.

When Jesus walked passed the tax table in Capernaum and took notice of Matthew, he looked at a man who was the chief of outcasts. Instead of condemning Matthew for his misdeeds, he simply said, "Follow me." The very same words he had addressed to the fishermen—Peter, Andrew, James, and John. How difficult it was for Matthew to believe his ears! Jesus was inviting *him*—a scoundrel and a traitor. Perhaps with a look of amazement, Matthew rose from the seat of customs and joined the band gathered around Jesus. Where was he to go? What was he to do? How was he to live? Matthew did not know the answers to any of these questions. He only knew that he would be with Jesus, and that was all he cared about.

Why did Jesus choose the hated Matthew? Because Jesus saw in Matthew possibilities that no one else, not even Matthew himself, imagined existed. Michelangelo, the immortal sculptor, once bought an ugly piece of marble that was gathering dust. When asked why he had bought such an inferior piece, he said, "Because there's an angel in there, and I've got to set it free." Jesus saw the hidden angel in Matthew. Jesus has X-ray vision in that he can see completely through us to what constitutes the "real" self. In calling Matthew Jesus challenged us to look closely at the hated and despised of the world for their unrealized potential. We choose the strong; Jesus chose the weak. We choose the rich; Jesus chose the poor. We choose the well; Jesus chose the sick. We choose the saints; Jesus chose the sinners. It is time we realize that God's grace is for all men. Our choosing must not be limited to any one group or class, but we must look for the hidden angel in all men.

Jesus was right about Matthew. His shield pictures three purses, which reminds us he was a redeemed tax collector. Perhaps the shield should have also pictured a pen, for Matthew wrote one of the greatest Gospels and so took his place as a hero among the apostles.

PRAYER   *O Almighty God, who by thy blessed Son didst call Matthew from the receipt of custom to be an Apostle and Evangelist; Grant us grace to forsake all covetous desires, and inordinate love of riches, and to follow the same thy Son Jesus Christ, who liveth and reigneth with thee and the Holy Ghost, one God, world without end. Amen.*

JAMES THE LESS AND JUDE

SCRIPTURE   James the son of Alphaeus, and Thaddaeus.
. . . (Matthew 10:3.)

MEDITATION   These two disciples appear as mystery men of the apostolic lists, coming to us as dim figures from the misty distance. They have the distinction of being the ninth and tenth disciples named in the Synoptic lists and the ones about whom we know least. They are surrounded by silence, and what we know of them can be summed up in a few sentences.

James the Less, son of Alphaeus, is hidden from view by two other men of the same name mentioned in the New Testament. One is James, brother of John, who was one of the foremost apostles. The other is James, brother of Jesus, who was probably the author of the New Testament epistle. His very nickname, "the Less," suggests his minor role. On his shield is a saw because, tradition says, he was thrown from the top of the Temple and his broken body was sawed asunder.

Jude—or Judas, the son of James—is called "trinomius" by Jerome, which means the man with three names. His other names give us a clue to his character. Lebbeus means courageous, hearty; while Thaddeus means lively, vivacious. Jude should not be confused with Judas, the traitor. The Fourth

118

Gospel makes the distinction clear when it records Jude asking a question of Jesus: "Judas (not Iscariot) said to him . . ." (14:22). Jude's shield is highlighted by a small sailing ship, symbolizing his missionary journeys. It is said that he went to Arabia, Syria, and Mesopotamia with the good news of Jesus Christ.

Jude and James the Less represent the truth that Christian faith can be spread by anonymous Christians whose names and deeds are hardly known. "Life is so daily," someone has complained. He was right. The days march by, and their feet seem to drag heavily. Life is common and humdrum for most of us. We will never have the opportunity to do the spectacular for the kingdom of God. Yet the battles are fought and won or lost in the common places of daily life. The most important deeds in Christian history have been wrought by people who were merely going about a daily task, trying to be good witnesses of Jesus Christ. Their names are unknown, overshadowed by the spectacular witnesses. Without anonymous Christians, however, there would be no great voices of truth. Who was reading the Preface to Luther's Epistle to the Romans that warmed Wesley's heart and set off the powder keg of revival in eighteenth-century England? No one knows. Who went to the ball park in Chicago and invited a ballplayer by the name of Billy Sunday to become a Christian? History does not record his name. Who were the people who led Wilfred Grenfell to become a missionary, or Harry Emerson Fosdick to enter the ministry, or the Rockefellers to use their money responsibly? These names do not readily come to mind. But don't doubt for a minute that they were vital witnesses!

Your life matters to God, no matter how small and insignificant it seems. Your daily, dull, prosaic life can be transformed into a vital witness for Christ. Nothing which is done in his Spirit—no matter how small it seems to us—is ever lost or wasted. As a pebble thrown into a lake causes ripples to spread in many different directions, so your life causes a chain reaction for good or evil. Someday someone will organize a group called Christians Anonymous—composed of people whose quiet, faithful witness is a mainstay to the church—and James and Jude will be the patron saints.

PRAYER   *Heavenly Father, thou dost love each one of us as if there were but one to love! All that we do is important in thy sight, and thou dost take our faithful deeds and use them for the consummation of thy kingdom. Make us willing to go about our tasks seeking only to glorify thee and caring that only one name be heard above all others, even Jesus Christ our Lord. Amen.*

SIMON THE ZEALOT

SCRIPTURE   Simon who was called the Zealot. . . . (Luke 6:15.)

Simon the Cananaean. . . . (Matt. 10:4.)

For just as the body is one and has many members, and

all the members of one body, though many, are one body, so it is with Christ. For by one Spirit we were all baptized into one body—Jews or Greeks, slaves or free—and all were made to drink of one Spirit. (I Cor. 12:12-13.)

MEDITATION   Simon the Zealot is mentioned only in the apostolic lists. The Bible gives us his name, but remains silent about other facets of his life. Yet his name is all we need to construct a fairly accurate picture about him. Shakespeare's Juliet asked:

> "What's in a name? that which we call a rose
> By any other name would smell as sweet."

In Simon's case a whole world of information is embodied in his name. Luke names him as "Simon who was called the Zealot." "Zealot" refers not to a family name, but to a political party which had many adherents among the Jewish people.

The Zealots were fanatical Jewish nationalists who would go to any lengths to preserve their ancient customs against the Romans. They had pledged themselves to the restoration of the old land, no matter what the cost. Violence was one of their main characteristics, and the movement degenerated into terrorism. Their hatred was so great that they plundered villages and killed their own people who had anything to do with the Romans.

Such was Simon the Zealot—a wild-eyed revolutionary, who hated the Roman invaders and anyone who dared to compromise with them as much as he loved Jewish custom and law. Yet his shield symbolizes that in the company of Jesus he became a new man. There is a fish lying on a book, the fish signifying that he was a fisher of men and the book

121

standing for the gospel. It is said that he was a frequent companion of Jude, the apostle who has a sailing ship on his shield. From murderer to missionary is a radical change in personality, but this is exactly what happened to Simon. Jesus taught him that hatred of persons—no matter how evil they are—is self-destructive and against God's law. He taught that God's love transcends national boundaries, coming to all men. As Paul came to realize years later, the church is one body, even though it is constructed of many members.

Like Simon, we face the danger of becoming militant nationalists who build walls around our shores and approach other nations in hate and fear. Our temptation is to turn the God of all nations into our national deity, whose job it is to assist us in winning wars, launching successful moon probes, and building bigger and better bombs to beat the Russians. Yet God comes before all the nations of the world as judge and redeemer. When we forget that God judges our national efforts and goals we become a potential threat to our own democratic way of life. The church today must resist efforts to be turned into a mouthpiece for the state, but must exercise a prophetic voice. The church must also recover once again the burning missionary zeal of the early Christians, pushing back our national boundaries and claiming responsibility for all the world as one.

PRAYER   *O Thou who art the light and the life of the world, have compassion, we pray thee, upon those who are sitting in darkness and in the shadow of death; and, as thou didst at the first, by the preaching of thine apostles, cause the light of thy gospel to shine throughout the world, be pleased to make thy ways known upon earth, thy saving health unto all nations. Bless*

*thy servants who have gone into hard fields and unto distant lands
to proclaim the message of salvation. Endue them with thy Holy
Spirit, enrich them with thy heavenly grace, prosper them in all
their labors. . . . And, O thou Lord of the harvest, we pray thee
to send forth more laborers into thy harvest. . . . And give us
grace to do our part in the great field of this world in sowing
and in reaping; through Jesus Christ. Amen.*

PAUL

SCRIPTURE   Paul, a servant of Jesus Christ, called to be an
apostle, set apart for the gospel of God. . . . (Rom. 1:1.)

For I am not ashamed of the gospel: It is the power of God
for salvation to every one who has faith, to the Jew first and
also to the Greek. For in it the righteousness of God is revealed
through faith for faith; as it is written, "He who through
faith is righteous shall live." (Rom. 1:16-17.)

MEDITATION   A watchword of another day was, "Away
with the theology of Paul and back to the religion of Jesus!"
It was fashionable to draw a sharp distinction between the two
and to accuse Paul of distorting Christ's teachings. We recognize, however, that Paul was a much more faithful witness

123

to the gospel than some gave him credit for being. He built bridges, not walls. Paul was the Moses of the early church, who led the covenant community out of the wilderness of confusion and into the promised land of the Spirit. Significantly, his shield shows an open Bible and a sword, symbolizing the word of God as "the sword of the Spirit."

A short man physically, Paul was tall enough spiritually to cast a long shadow down through the centuries. The rediscovery of Paul led to the Protestant Reformation. Luther spoke from Paul's understanding of the faith when he said, "Here I stand, I cannot do otherwise!" John Wesley felt his heart strangely warmed while listening to *Luther's Preface to the Commentary on the Epistle of Romans,* and the religious revival that swept England was born. In our century Karl Barth's romance with Romans has challenged the church to re-examine the roots of its faith. What is the secret of Paul's influence? It is summarized in the first chapter of Romans.

Paul was a servant of Jesus Christ. Once an enthusiastic persecutor of the church, he was confronted by the claims of Christ in a dramatic way on the Damascus Road. He realized that in the name of truth he had been persecuting truth. So he became a servant of Jesus Christ. He came to Christ, laying no claims upon him, not even for forgiveness. He approached Christ as a servant approaches his master, in absolute trust and obedience. The master ordered; the servant carried out the command. The servant was bound to his master, and thus became a member of a new household with special responsibilities and privileges. Paul no longer belonged to himself, but to the God who revealed himself in Christ. We, too, must understand our relationship to Jesus Christ in this way.

Paul was called to be an apostle. This great preacher's

power did not come from himself—his own talents, skills, and abilities—but from God's mighty act of calling. God calls man, and man responds. Paul was not forced by divine edict to become an apostle, he was merely called. He could have responded negatively, but by saying yes to God's call Paul was lifted to new levels of action. So it is that God's call comes today. God calls us into the fellowship of the church; he calls us to be responsible in our work and to serve our neighbors. We must never forget that what power we have comes from God's call, and not from our own ability.

Paul was set apart for the gospel of God, and he was not ashamed of it. At the center of the Christian gospel is a scandal—the cross of Jesus Christ. Paul himself called Christ crucified "a stumbling-block to Jews and folly to Gentiles." He does not stop with this, however. "To those who are called . . . Christ [is] the power of God and the wisdom of God" (I Cor. 1:23-24). In the suffering, crucified, and risen Lord God is at work to reconcile the world to himself. This is the gospel which Paul proclaimed unashamedly: God comes to sinful man in Jesus Christ and sets him free from his sins to a new life of faith. It is good, great, glorious news!

PRAYER *O God, who through the preaching of thy servant Paul has made us aware of our sins and our need of reconciliation, grant that we may recognize that thou art willing to forgive us and restore us to thyself; in the name of him who brings new life, even Jesus Christ our Lord. Amen.*

MARY, THE MOTHER OF JESUS

SCRIPTURE   My soul magnifies the Lord,
and my spirit rejoices in God my Savior,
for he has regarded the low estate of his hand-
maiden.
For behold, henceforth all generations will call
me blessed;
for he who is mighty has done great things for me,
and holy is his name. (Luke 1:46-49.)

MEDITATION   Several symbols are associated with Mary,
the mother of Jesus. There is a crescent moon which refers
to her glory, reminiscent of Jesus Christ as "the Sun of
Righteousness." Another symbol is the rose, which is also used
to remind us of the messianic promise. The fleur-de-lis represents her purity, in addition to standing for the Trinity.
More symbols are used to represent Mary than any other New
Testament character save Jesus Christ himself.

Protestants really don't know what to make of Mary. The
Roman Catholic Church, elevating Mary far above her place
in the gospel tradition, has made Protestants respond in a
negative way. We have shoved her into the background in
reaction to what we consider an inappropriate emphasis. It's
high time that we develop a Protestant appreciation of Mary,

realizing that she is a symbol of womanhood at its best and deserves an honored place in our thinking. What are some of her outstanding characteristics?

She sought to do the will of the Lord as it was revealed unto her. Mary was a woman of faith. She was visited by an angel and, although she was a virgin, was told she was going to bear a child. What was her final response? "Behold I am the handmaid of the Lord; let it be to me according to your word" (Luke 1:38). This was the response of faith. Mary was saying to God, "I am open to your visitation. Thy will be done in my life."

Mary's life was a symphony of wondrous joy. The song she sang, the Magnificat, is a glorious hymn of praise to Almighty God. It is a turning of the soul toward the Creator, an ecstatic uttering of the deepest part of a person. There is no trace of personal pride in this song, but the realization of her "low estate." Generations will "call her blessed," not because she has done anything herself, but because God has acted in her life to do great things. No wonder her life was punctuated with exclamation points of joy!

Mary was with Jesus from the first to the last. She took her vocation as a mother with profound seriousness. Although she misunderstood Jesus, and, on at least one occasion, came to bring him back home with her in order to keep him from preaching his disturbing message, she loved him as only a mother could. As Jesus' ministry grew, she began to understand what he meant when he said that whoever did his will was his mother. Doubtless at some point in her life she became more than a mother to Jesus. She became a follower, devoted to the coming kingdom. Even when they hung him upon a cruel cross to die, Mary was there. She stood beneath the cross, both as a follower and as his mother. Jesus beheld his mother from the cross, thereby paying her a lasting tribute of love.

PRAYER   *O Lord of life and home, we pray thee for purity of heart. May we dwell together in our family as sons and daughters of thine. Give us courage for the living of these days and an abiding love for all peoples. Keep us uncomfortable until all are comfortable, and hungry until all are fed. We do not ask for safety, but for salvation through Jesus Christ. Amen.*

JOHN THE BAPTIST

SCRIPTURE   John the baptizer appeared in the wilderness, preaching a baptism of repentance for the forgiveness of sins. And there went out to him all the country of Judea, and all the people of Jerusalem; and they were baptized by him in the river Jordan, confessing their sins. Now John was clothed with camel's hair, and had a leather girdle around his waist, and ate locusts and wild honey. And he preached, saying, "After me comes he who is mightier than I, the thong of whose sandals I am not worthy to stoop down and untie. I have baptized you with water; but he will baptize you with the Holy Spirit." (Mark 1:4-8.)

MEDITATION   If John the Baptist were to appear in our day he would be labeled a "beatnik" or a religious fanatic. Imagine a bearded man walking down our streets dressed in a camel's hair coat—which is his symbol—with a girdle hugging his waist, living only on honey and locusts, and preaching a gospel of repentance! Quite possibly he would land in jail or be placed under psychiatric examination. Even to his own day and to his own people he was an enigma. The Hebrews, who were not without prophets in their colorful history, had never seen anyone exactly like John. Despite his unusual appearance, he converted many people to his band. Jesus paid him a great compliment: "I tell you, among those born of women none is greater than John" (Luke 7:28). Why was John the Baptist great?

John was great because he knew that there was one greater. He recognized that he was only a small candle bearing witness to the true light that enlightens every man. Holding a right opinion of himself, John the Baptist was not haughty, proud, puffed-up, or impressed with his own importance. He understood himself to be an instrument in the hands of a greater power, being used as one who prepares the way for another. In the Middle Ages, when the king entered, trumpeters would sound a note announcing his coming. No trumpeter thought himself more important than the king. This was the relationship John the Baptist had to Jesus Christ. John gathered disciples only to instruct them about one who was coming, and it is evident that after his death most of his disciples joined themselves to Jesus. It takes a great man to have a right self-image, humbly accepting the role of a preparer.

129

John was great for another reason. He fearlessly proclaimed righteousness in the midst of overwhelming evil. Herod had married his brother's wife, which was considered a black crime by the Jews. John dared face Herod and told him plainly that it was not lawful for him to marry Herodias. This prophetic witness led finally to his arrest, imprisonment, and death. If we had been in John's sandals we would have doubtlessly skirted a direct clash. We would have reasoned, "Better not to create any trouble. God will punish Herod in his good time. I have enough to do taking care of my own life." But John realized that God chooses men through whom he speaks his word of judgment and redemption, and if they refuse to speak the word is often never heard. Risking all for the kingdom he knew was coming in Jesus Christ, John summoned courage to be faithful to his prophetic mission.

In the final analysis, all Christians are called to be preparers—voices crying in the wilderness of life. Our message is the same as John's: "Prepare the way of the Lord, make his paths straight. Repent, for the kingdom of heaven is at hand. He comes who will baptize with the Holy Spirit and who is mightier than all."

PRAYER   *O God, who revealest thyself through prophets and poets and who most fully spoke to man in the revelation of thy Son Jesus Christ, make us mindful of our call to witness courageously to him, to straighten crooked paths, and to work for righteousness which is the climate of thy kingdom. Amen.*

STEPHEN

SCRIPTURE   But they cried out with a loud voice and stopped their ears and rushed together upon him. Then they cast him out of the city and stoned him; and the witnesses laid down their garments at the feet of a young man named Saul. And as they were stoning Stephen, he prayed, "Lord Jesus, receive my spirit." And he knelt down and cried with a loud voice, "Lord, do not hold this sin against them." And when he had said this, he fell asleep. And Saul was consenting to his death. (Acts 7:57–8:1.)

MEDITATION   Young Stephen, deacon of the church, was stoned to death at the hands of an angry mob. Actually, the mob had been acting as judges in a court of Jewish law. Stephen had been brought before them to answer charges of blasphemy. His trouble was that he presented too good a defense. Tracing the disobedience of Israel down through its history, Stephen hotly charged, "You stiff-necked people, uncircumcised in heart and ears, you always resist the Holy Spirit. As your fathers did, so do you" (vs. 51). His judges then became his jury and his executioners. In their rage, they stoned him to death—a manner of execution reserved for only the foulest crimes. Stephen's symbol is a coat and three stones.

But the manner of Stephen's dying was more important than anyone could possibly know, even those devoted Christians who came for his broken body and buried it with great

131

mourning. As his Master had, Stephen died with a whispered prayer of forgiveness for his persecutors on his lips. He died with his face toward heaven, content in the faith that God would receive his spirit. He died as a man of faith who could face the future—no matter what it might be—with trust and confidence because he had found new life in Jesus Christ. The way Stephen died moved something deep inside one of the mob, a man named Saul who held the garments of the mob. What happened to Saul was imperceptible, yet it was very real. Stephen's stoning set off a whole chain of events in Saul's life that led to his becoming a new man in Christ. Saul became Paul, the architect of early Christian thought.

The change in Saul's life did not come immediately, for he was "stiff-necked" and closed to the truth. After Stephen's death he went on a rampage against the Christians. Acts 9:1 describes his zeal: "But Saul, still breathing threats and murder against the disciples of the Lord, went to the high priest and asked him for letters to the synagogues at Damascus, so that if he found any belonging to the Way, men or women, he might bring them bound to Jerusalem." On his way to Damascus, Saul confronted the Lord in a unique way. This was not the first time he had been confronted, however. In Stephen Jesus Christ had spoken to Saul. On the Damascus Road Jesus Christ was speaking another word. Without the dying witness of Stephen there is doubt whether the encounter on the road would have meant anything at all to Saul.

Stephen was the first Christian martyr, but he was not the last. In every age Christians have been called upon to give their "last full measure of devotion" for the sake of Christ. In every age Stephen will be remembered as one who gave us an example of how to witness unto the death.

PRAYER   *Grant, O Lord, that, in all our sufferings here upon earth for the testimony of thy truth, we may stedfastly look up to heaven, and by faith behold the glory that shall be revealed; and, being filled with the Holy Ghost, may learn to love and bless our persecutors by the example of thy first Martyr Saint Stephen, who prayed for his murderers to thee, O blessed Jesus, who standest at the right hand of God to succour all those who suffer for thee, our only Mediator and Advocate. Amen.*

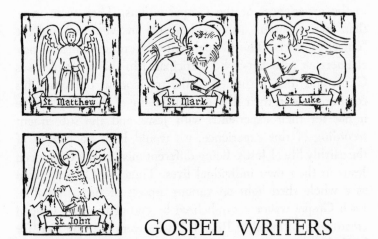

GOSPEL WRITERS

SCRIPTURE   But as for you, continue in what you have learned and have firmly believed, knowing from whom you learned it and how from childhood you have been acquainted with the sacred writings which are able to instruct you for salvation through faith in Christ Jesus. All scripture is inspired by God and profitable for teaching, for reproof, for correction, and for training in righteousness, that the man of God may be complete, equipped for every good work. (II Tim. 3:14-17.)

This is the disciple who is bearing witness to these things, and who has written these things; and we know that his testimony is true. (John 21:24.)

MEDITATION   The Gospel writers have often been compared with reporters who witnessed the same events, but wrote about what they saw in a different way. This helps to explain the differences between the Gospels, but it does not do justice to the experiences of the Gospel writers. They were more than mere reporters who stood outside an event and told the "objective" facts. The Gospel writers were announcers, proclaimers, or preachers who participated in the event of Jesus Christ and then witnessed to the tremendous difference his coming made in their lives and in the life of the world. Were it not for their experience with Jesus and the subsequent recording of this experience, we would have no picture of the earthly life of Jesus. Being different men, they experienced Jesus in their own individual lives. Thus the Gospels taken as a whole shed light on various aspects of his personality. Each Gospel writer is symbolized by one of the four winged creatures mentioned in Rev. 4:7, who were praising God for his holiness.

Matthew is portrayed by a winged man. This is because his Gospel begins with the human genealogy of our Lord and emphasizes his manhood throughout. Reading Matthew, we are reminded that Jesus Christ was "wholly man." He knew the sweat of work on his brow and the dust of the earth on his feet. He grew hungry and thirsty and tired. Whenever the humanity of Jesus is lost his divinity stands in danger of decay.

Mark is represented by a winged lion. The lion is said to signify royalty, and thus Mark stresses the kingly office of Christ. Christ is king in this Gospel. He exercises control over demons and sickness. Although he wants to keep his messiahship secret, it is obvious to his closest disciples that he is the one who is sent from God.

Luke is symbolized by a winged calf because his Gospel most fully treats the sacrifice of Christ. A calf or ox is the most common symbol of sacrifice. One of the most difficult facts which the early disciples had to face was the crucifixion of Jesus. Its immediate result was the shattering of their precious dreams about him. But they grew to understand that the crucifixion was the climax of God's love for them. In grateful response to Christ's sacrifice they went forth to sacrifice themselves for the good news which he was.

John's emblem is the eagle. This bird, said to soar higher than any other, is used because John sketches the divine nature of Christ in the most sublime terms of all the Gospel writers. Listen to the way in which he begins his Gospel:

In the beginning was the Word, and the Word was with God, and the Word was God. He was in the beginning with God; and all things were made through him, and without him was not anything made that was made. . . . And the Word became flesh and dwelt among us, full of grace and truth; we have beheld his glory, glory as of the only Son from the Father. (1:1-3, 14.)

135

PRAYER   *Almighty God, who hast revealed thyself through the witness of the Gospel writers, we give thee thanks for the good news delivered to us. Grant that we may hear thy word and respond in all faithfulness when it is read and preached; through Jesus Christ, the light of the world. Amen.*

VI

MEDITATIONS ON SYMBOLS
OF BIBLICAL DOCTRINES

STAR
OF BETHLEHEM

SCRIPTURE   Now when Jesus was born in Bethlehem of
Judea in the days of Herod the king, behold, wise men from
the East came to Jerusalem, saying, "Where is he who has
been born king of the Jews? For we have seen his star in the
East, and have come to worship him." . . . Lo, the star which
they had seen in the East went before them, till it came to rest
over the place where the child was. When they saw the star,
they rejoiced exceedingly with great joy; and going into the
house they saw the child with Mary his mother, and they fell
down and worshiped him. Then, opening their treasures, they
offered him gifts, gold and frankincense and myrrh. (Matt.
2:1-2, 9*b*-11.)

MEDITATION   There are billions and billions of stars in the
universe, constantly being made and disintegrating to dust.
In the Christian story, however, there is only one star—the
star which faithfully guided the Magi to the newborn Christ
Child. It shines brightly in Matthew's Gospel, and on top
of our Christmas trees hang tiny replicas of the star of
Bethlehem. Down through the centuries this strange star has

captured the adoration of the faithful and the imagination of the poets.

Despite popular use, the star as a Christian symbol is related to the season of Epiphany, not Christmas. The star led the Gentiles—"wise men from the East"—to the newborn Babe and thus announced to the whole world that the Christ was born. The word "Epiphany" really means "manifestation or showing," which describes what the star did. By the star God led men to Christ.

In Maxwell Anderson's play *Lost in the Stars* one of the characters sings:

> Each one lives alone
>   In a world of dark,
> Crossing the skies
>   In a lonely arc,
> Save when love leaps out like a leaping spark
>   Over thousands, thousands of miles.

Anderson put his finger on the great announcement of the star to man: Love had leaped out like a leaping spark over thousands and thousands of miles! The Apostle John said of Christ, "In him was life, and the life was the light of men. The light shines in darkness, and the darkness has not overcome it" (1:4-5). The star of Bethlehem apparently disappeared into the darkness of the heavens when its task was accomplished, but the light which came in Jesus Christ shines forever and ever. Darkness cannot destroy this light, for to the light belongs final victory. In this world we know the darkness of evil, oppression, violence, dictatorship, injustice, and sickness, but the light shines in this darkness and is not overcome.

How can we know the Reality to whom the star pointed? The Magi, who lived alone in a world of dark until the spark leaped into their lives, sensed the answer. They lifted up their eyes to the heavens, to the direction from which they thought God's truth would come. When they saw the star they had faith that God sent it to guide them to a newborn king. So they followed the star. We, too, know the Reality when we lift our eyes from the level of complacency and self-seeking and, without counting the cost, follow the star wherever it leads. In the Gospel lesson Matthew tells us that the star leads us to the Christ.

PRAYER   *O Thou who art the true sun of the world, ever rising, and never going down, who by thy most wholesome appearing and light dost nourish and make joyful all things in heaven and in earth; we beseech thee mercifully to shine into our hearts, that the night and darkness of sin and the mists of error on every side may be driven away, and that all our life long we may walk without stumbling as children of the light and the day. Amen.*

TORCH

SCRIPTURE   You are the light of the world. A city set on a hill cannot be hid. Nor do men light a lamp and put it under a bushel, but on a stand, and it gives light to all in the house. Let your light so shine before men, that they may see your good works and give glory to your Father who is in heaven. (Matt. 5:14-16.)

Beware of practicing your piety before men in order to be seen by them; for then you will have no reward from your Father who is in heaven. (Matt. 6:1.)

MEDITATION   A torch symbolizes the Christian responsibility to witness and immediately calls to mind the famous command of Jesus to let our lights shine before men. When Christ calls a man he bids him to come and be a light. Jesus did not say, "You must be the light of the world," or even "You will become the light of the world." He said, "You *are* the light of the world." In other words, "This is a present reality in your lives because you have accepted my call to discipleship."

After entering into a new relationship with Christ we have no other choice than to be a light. It is part and parcel of our discipleship. We are cities set on a hill, which cannot be hid. We are lamps whose duty it is to give light to all the house and not to be hid under a bushel. Nor is the light of our own making, for in ourselves alone is darkness. The light which we let shine before men is the light which we receive from Christ, who is the light of the world. It is the light shining from the cross, a light of self-sacrifice and service to others.

Yet there is a startling shift in mood between the fifth and sixth chapters of Matthew. At first we think that these chapters cannot stand together, but then we understand that they cannot stand apart. They logically follow one another, forming a precious paradox. Let your light shine before men, but "beware of practicing your piety before men in order to be seen by them." The Christan community is to be visible, yet hidden. Our lights are to shine before men, not in order that they may see us, but that they may find the Father who is in heaven. We often work too hard at being unique and visible, thereby becoming religious salesmen instead of disciples. We often need, not to draw attention to the Christian character of our works, but to quietly go about our duty.

Sören Kierkegaard had a word about the hiddenness of Christian discipleship. He imagined finding a Knight of Faith, a true representative of the Christian man. When he found him Kierkegaard leapt back in surprise: "Good God! Is this really he? Why, he looks like an Inspector of Taxes!" An ordinary citizen! This is the insight of Matt. 6:1—the disciple is often hidden. But it is also true—and this is the first part of our paradox—that the Knight of Faith will not only appear hidden as an Inspector of Taxes, but will be visible as a Knight of Faith. Proclaiming a valid Christian witness is essentially keeping a balance between visibility and hiddenness, between being a Knight of Faith and an Inspector of Taxes.

143

PRAYER   *Send us, O God, as thy messengers to hearts without a home, to lives without love, to the crowds without a guide. Send us to the children whom none have blessed, to the famished whom none have visited, to the fallen whom none have lifted, to the bereaved whom none have comforted. Kindle thy flame on the altars of our hearts, that others may be warmed thereby; cause thy light to shine in our souls, that others may see the way; keep our sympathies and insight ready, our wills keen, our hands quick to help our brothers in their need; through Jesus Christ our Lord. Amen.*

ANCHOR

SCRIPTURE   Why are you cast down, O my soul,
            and why are you disquieted within me?
        Hope in God; for I shall again praise him,
            my help and my God. (Ps. 42:5.)

We have this as a sure and steadfast anchor of the soul, a hope that enters into the inner shrine behind the curtain, where Jesus has gone as a forerunner on our behalf. (Heb. 6:19-20.)

MEDITATION   The anchor as a symbol for hope was used

frequently in the catacombs by persecuted Christians. They were men and women for whom the light of day had been snuffed out by the Roman authorities, but who were finding a more enduring light in their hope. Another symbol—closely related to this one—is the anchor cross, combining both an anchor and a cross. Like the fish symbol, this disguised cross hid its true significance from persecutors. The anchor of hope held Christians' faith secure, although they were threatened on every hand by dark, angry waters. In what do Christians hope?

Christians hope in the God of Jesus Christ. Hope in him, and him alone, is the only sure anchor. Christian faith is not founded on anything man has done, or can do, for himself. It is founded on what God has done in Jesus Christ. The shallow optimism of the nineteenth century turned into the bitter grapes of World War I. Today, there is increasing evidence that man's capacity to achieve power is outstripping his ability to control it. Once again we need to be reminded that Jesus Christ is the "hope of the world." Man's placing hope in himself, and not in God, is the essence of his sin and his predicament. Without God our striving is losing and our dreams are doomed to become nightmares.

Christians hope in the present salvation of man. God comes to man in the present, not in some far-off past or distant future. Our main problem with faith is that we have tried to freeze God in the historical Jesus or limit him to coming in the last judgment, forgetting that his mercy and judgment confront man in the present tense. Hope, if it is genuine, must always be considered as hope for today. The real question for the Christian is, What difference does Christ make to man now? The gospel answers as a herald of hope: In whatever situation you find yourself, God is in that situation offering wholeness. The anchor cross symbolizes God's suffering love as a conquering love that can make all our sunsets sunrises and all our midnights high noons—*now*.

Christians hope in the resurrection of the body. Physical death is a future event for man, yet it holds over us such a sway in its inevitability that one psychologist said that, at its base, all fear is the fear of dying. Nor are any of us removed from experiencing death in our circle of family and friends. Shelley painted a word picture of our finitude:

> Death is here and death is there,
> Death is busy everywhere,
> All around, within, beneath,
> Above is death—and we are death.

That man must die—this is acknowledged by our Christian faith. There is another chapter to be written, however, and its author is God. We believe that as God has been faithful to us in our living, so he will be faithful to us in our dying. As we are "in Christ" and are buried in a death like his, so we shall know the glory of his resurrection.

PRAYER   *O God of all hope, deliver us from despair. We pray for grace to see thee active in all the events of life—even those events which tear at our faith and make us tremble. We thank thee that thou hast not left us alone in the universe, but hast come to us in Jesus Christ and dost meet us at every corner in thy Holy Spirit. May we find in thee our help and our hope. Amen.*

SHIELD

SCRIPTURE   Stand therefore ... above all taking the shield of faith, with which you can quench all the flaming darts of the evil one. (Eph. 6:14*a*, 16.)

But now the righteousness of God has been manifested apart from law, although the law and the prophets bear witness to it, the righteousness of God through faith in Jesus Christ for all who believe. For there is no distinction; since all have sinned and fall short of the glory of God, they are justified by his grace as a gift. (Rom. 3:21-24*a*.)

MEDITATION   A shield bearing the Latin cross stands for faith or trust. It alludes to Paul's reference in Ephesians to the "whole armor of God." The Christian soldier is to wear the girdle of truth, the breastplate of righteousness, the sandals of peace, the helmet of salvation, the sword of the Spirit—and, above all, the shield of faith. Paul, of course, was not referring to protection from physical evils in this scripture passage, but rather to the evils which work on the inner man. Exactly how does faith help us live victoriously?

God, through the gift of faith, gives us his presence. Often people ask, "How do I know that God is for me, not against me? Life is so filled with tragedy." We are given assurance that God is for us, not by mental gymnastics, not by trying to feel his presence, but by the living God himself who comes to us in all of life. It is God's presence that sustains the Christian in the hour of deepest need and makes him exclaim with the Apostle Paul, "Who shall separate us from the love of Christ? Shall tribulation or distress, or persecution, or famine, or nakedness, or peril, or sword? . . . No, in all these things we are more than conquerors through him who loved us" (Rom. 8:35, 37). In Jesus Christ God acted decisively to assure man of his continual love.

God, through the gift of faith, gives us his power. The God we worship is no weakling, unable to finish the work of love he has started. When we are in the presence of God we are with a strong friend. No matter what hardship may befall us, our family, our friends, or our nation, we know that God's purpose ultimately will triumph. Robert Stopford, one of Nelson's commanders, after telling of many hardships and trials, exclaimed, "We were half-starved, and otherwise inconvenienced by being so long out of port. But our reward was—we were with Nelson." The Christian's reward is his fellowship with God, who through the resurrection of Christ has shown us that his love conquers all, even the last enemy known as death.

God, through the gift of faith, gives us his peace. Paul speaks of the "peace of God, which passes all understanding." It is a deep lasting peace, not like the palliatives which the world offers. One of the great problems of our day is that men are settling for sugarcoated hell, forgetting that the sugarcoating soon melts away. The peace which God gives is found in involvement in life. The New Testament teaches us that we find our deepest peace in the service of God and of our neighbor. Look around you and you will discover that the worried, insecure, restless, confused, torn, neurotic people are those who have turned in upon themselves to find life's meaning; while the peaceful, well-balanced, healthy, whole people are those who have turned out to serve.

PRAYER

O God, our help in ages past,
Our hope for years to come,
Our shelter from the stormy blast,
And our eternal home!

Under the shadow of Thy throne
Still may we dwell secure;
Sufficient is Thine arm alone,
And our defense is sure.

Before the hills in order stood,
Or earth received her frame,
From everlasting Thou art God,
To endless years the same.

. . . .

Our God, our help in ages past,
Our hope for years to come;
Be Thou our guide while life shall last,
And our eternal home! Amen.
—Isaac Watts

SHIP

SCRIPTURE   For just as the body is one and has many members, and all members of the body, though many, are one body, so it is with Christ. For by one Spirit we were all baptized into one body—Jews or Greeks, slaves or free—and all were made to drink of one Spirit. (I Cor. 12:12.)

MEDITATION   In Christian art the church is shown as a ship. Today some denominations call the main body of their churches the nave, a word which comes from the Latin word, *navis,* meaning ship. It is an apt symbol because the church is the ship on which we sail across the sea of life. By comparing the church with a ship, we come to a better understanding of its nature and significance.

A ship has a captain. It is the captain's duty to chart a course for the ship and to keep it on that course. When on the high seas, the captain's word is law to both the crew and the passengers. To rebel against captain's orders is mutiny and is punishable by execution. In like manner, the church has a captain—Jesus Christ. New Testament writers referred to Jesus as the head of the church. The church looks to him for its course and directions, as the crew of a ship looks its captain. Long ago he gave us our course: To be a servant community, responsible to him as Lord. In the centuries of church history we have veered far off course many times; yet the course is charted, and we know in what direction we should be going.

Because Jesus Christ is the Lord of the church, the church will endure eternally. The winds of the world cannot destroy the church or keep it from finally accomplishing its mission.

A ship affords protection. We could not swim the Atlantic from New York to England, but great ocean liners make the voyage daily. Ships offer protection from the waters below and the storms above. So it is with the church. Christians are protected from life's storms. This does not mean that they are not exposed to them like all human beings. Of course they are! But there is a difference in these experiences because of their faith. All events of life can be accepted as working together for good, since God lives and visits us. God is never ultimately frustrated. To this the church bears witness. So the Christian makes this affirmation about life: "We are handicapped on all sides, but we are never frustrated; we are puzzled, but never in despair. We are persecuted, but we never have to stand it alone: we may be knocked down but we are never knocked out!" (II Cor. 4:8-9, Phillips).

A ship offers adventure. There is a high thrill about a sea voyage, and the lure of sailing has captured more than one man. On a ship man—a land animal—is put in a new environment, one which promises him great adventure. The church calls us to a life of adventure too. Unlike most ships, there is no room for passengers in the church. No one should come aboard "just for the ride." The church is a battleship and calls for a crew ready and willing to fight. Our work is never finished, for the enemies of Christ's kingdom are strong and assume many different faces. Today the church must understand its nature as a battleship. It must come out of its moorings, take to the high seas, do battle, and claim all the world —both sea and land—for Jesus Christ our Lord.

PRAYER   *We beseech thee, O merciful God, to visit the church with thy Holy Spirit so that it may be a strong ship of salvation for the whole world. Renew the church's prophetic zeal and hate of injustice. Guide our course through the perilous waters of our day, for we are threatened on every hand by secularism and idolatry. Make us aware of the tasks which thou dost call us to perform in these days. May we have done with lesser things, and give our hearts and minds and souls and strength to serve the King of kings. Amen.*

WHEAT AND GRAPES

SCRIPTURE   Now as they were eating, Jesus took bread, and blessed, and broke it, and gave it to the disciples and said, "Take, eat; this is my body." And he took a cup, and when he had given thanks he gave it to them, saying, "Drink of it, all of you; for this is my blood of the covenant, which is poured out for many for the forgiveness of sins." (Matt. 26:26-28.)

The cup of blessing which we bless, is it not a participation in the blood of Christ? The bread which we break, is it not a participation in the body of Christ? Because there is one loaf, we who are many are one body, for we all partake of the same loaf. (I Cor. 10:16-17, R.S.V.)

MEDITATION   Whenever we see wheat or grapes on a stained-glass window we are reminded of the fellowship meal of the Christian community, the Lord's Supper or Holy Communion. There has not been a single Sunday since the church was born, almost two thousand years ago, that this meal has not been observed in countless congregations the world over. Some churches celebrate the meal every Sunday, others once a month, still others once a year during Lent. Whatever the practice, the meal is accompanied by reverence, awe, and anticipation. In the text from Corinthians, Paul gives us valuable insight into the meaning of the Lord's Supper for Christians.

When we celebrate this fellowship meal we participate in the body and blood of Christ. The Lord's Supper speaks to us of the death of Christ as symbolized in the elements of bread and wine. Christians who come, however unworthily, are challenged to participate in a sacrificial life which is poured out for others. The cross, as the symbol of Christ's sacrifice, is stamped upon the fellowship meal, but the Lord's Supper does not end with the death of Jesus Christ. It symbolizes participation in his resurrection. As we have died a death like his, so shall we be raised to a life like his. The celebration of fellowship meal is a time for making promises; it is a time of dying to the old man and of becoming alive to Christ. New life—this is precisely what is offered us in this holy meal. Nor must we ever forget that we come to this meal in utter dependence upon God. It is he who has laid the table. He is our host. Participation in the body and blood of Christ is not dependent upon our works, but upon God's graciousness in Jesus Christ. He comes to us before we ever think of going to him. This is what is meant by "prevenient grace."

Again, Paul suggests that whenever we celebrate the Lord's Supper we are molded together in community. The Lord's Supper is like marriage. In marriage a man and woman are lifted out of themselves and become "one flesh." They are no longer two, but one. Through the Lord's Supper an entire community of faith is lifted out of itself, and the many become one. Not only do we participate on a vertical level—with the God in Christ—but we participate on a horizontal level—with our neighbors, in whom God is certainly present. In the early church one loaf of bread was used in the service. The minister broke the loaf of bread into pieces and gave to the communicants. Thus all shared from one loaf, symbolizing their oneness in Christ. So it is that God calls us to oneness as a church and as a world in this fellowship meal.

PRAYER   *We give thanks to thee, our Father, for the Holy Vine of David thy child, which, thou didst make known to us through Jesus thy child; to thee be glory forever. We give thee thanks, our Father, for the life and knowledge which thou didst make known to us through Jesus thy child. To thee be glory forever. As this broken bread was scattered upon the mountains, but was brought together and became one, so let thy church be gathered together from the ends of the earth into thy kingdom, for thine is the glory and the power through Jesus Christ forever. Amen.*

154

CENSER AND HARP

SCRIPTURE   Rejoice in the Lord, O you righteous!
                 Praise befits the upright.
                 Praise the Lord with the lyre,
                     make melody to him with the harp of
                     ten strings! (Ps. 33:1-3.)
                 I was glad when they said to me,
                 "Let us go to the house of the Lord!"
                                              (Ps. 122:1.)

MEDITATION   Worship and praise stand at the very heart of the Christian faith. When we hear the voice of him who challenges our self-understanding, who is above all and in all and through all, our natural response is to "worship and bow down." When we hear the word which he speaks—the word of forgiveness and love in Jesus Christ—our only response can be praise. He has been good to us beyond our deserving, and faithful to us even though we have been unfaithful to him.

The censer and the harp stand, respectively, for worship and praise. In earliest times the censer was used in the worship service as a container for sweet-smelling incense, while the harp is thought of as an instrument of praise. This symbol is especially appropriate on exposed organ pipes or on choir

155

benches. Censer and harp go together as symbols, for as there can be no true worship without praise; the very act of praise involves worship. What does it mean to worship as Christians?

Worship means to acknowledge God as the one to whom our total allegiance belongs. We find worth in many places—in the face of a friend, in the beauty of a sunset, in the excitement of a sport. Yet ultimate worth—the center around which life is built and finds its meaning—is none other than the God who reveals himself in Jesus Christ and calls us to himself. Of course we fail time and again to build our lives around God, choosing instead false gods. We are idolaters; we divide our loyalties and are unfaithful. In the service of worship, however, we come together and affirm once again that we believe God is our ultimate worth. We confess that we have been unfaithful, and we beg forgiveness. We open up our lives to receive his forgiveness and his redeeming word which comes to us through hymns, prayers, scriptures, and sermons. As a final act, we offer up our lives to God, asking that we might be faithful in praising and serving him.

Worship is the highest act of our "life together." In short, worship is corporate in nature. This does not discount the fact that private devotions are worship and that worship can take place outside the church building. But private and "outside" worship is dependent upon our public and "inside" worship. There can be no life without community, and no vital Christianity exists without community. We come together as believers, as the Body of Christ, to praise, confess, listen, and dedicate our lives. We receive strength from one another's profession of faith, and God comes to us in our neighbor's worship. As John Wesley said, "There is no such thing as a solitary Christian." So may the censer and harp remind us of the high opportunity which we have to worship together in spirit and in truth.

PRAYER   *O Thou in whom we live, and move, and have our being, thou hast come as a light in the midst of our darkness, as life in the midst of our death, as power in the midst of our weakness. We come before thy presence with singing. We enter into thy gates with thanksgiving and into thy courts with praise. We give thanks unto thee for thy goodness and truth and everlasting mercy. Grant that, praising thee, we may love thee and that, loving thee, we may serve thee in the way which Christ revealed. Amen.*

REFERENCES

Page	Line	
27	26	From *The Book of Common Prayer*, p. 67.
33	16	Adapted from *The Kingdom, the Power and the Glory*, p. 26, by permission of Oxford University Press.
37	10	Story from Alice M. Brookman, *My Own Work Book on Christian Symbolism* (New York: Morehouse-Gorham Company, 1940).
44	6	From *The Book of Common Prayer*, p. 6.
63	8	From Walter Russell Bowie, *Lift Up Your Hearts* (Nashville: Abingdon Press, 1956), p. 60.
72	12	Prayer for the Lambeth Conference, 1948.
77	23	Adapted from *The Book of Worship for Church and Home*, p. 203.

85	16	Adapted from *The Book of Common Prayer*, p. 157.
90	14	From Marc Connelly, *The Green Pastures.* Used by permission of the author.
94	11	From *The Book of Worship for Church and Home*, p. 180.
99	9	Søren Kierkegaard.
109	12	From *The Book of Common Prayer*, p. 254.
112	5	From *The Book of Common Prayer*, p. 249.
117	10	From *The Book of Common Prayer*, p. 250.
122	25	From *The Book of Worship for Church and Home*, pp. 135-36.
133	1	From *The Book of Common Prayer*, pp. 99-100.
140	12	Copyright © 1946 by DeSylva, Brown & Henderson, Inc., New York, N. Y.
141	12	From *The Book of Worship for Church and Home*, pp. 162-63.
144	1	From *Prayers Old and New* (5th ed.; Forward Movement of the Episcopal Church, 1943), p. 75.